KINGS
Come
FORTH

KINGS
Come
FORTH

GARY J. BORGSTEDE

EXcel
BOOKS
A STRANG COMPANY

Most STRANG COMMUNICATIONS BOOK GROUP products are available at special quantity discounts for bulk purchase for sales promotions, premiums, fund-raising, and educational needs. For details, write Strang Communications Book Group, 600 Rinehart Road, Lake Mary, Florida 32746, or telephone (407) 333-0600.

KINGS COME FORTH! by Gary Borgstede
Published by Excel Books, A Strang Company
600 Rinehart Road, Lake Mary, Florida 32746
www.strangbookgroup.com

Unless otherwise noted, all Scripture quotations are from the New King James Version of the Bible. Copyright © 1979, 1980, 1982 by Thomas Nelson, Inc., publishers. Used by permission.

Scripture quotations marked NLT are from the Holy Bible, New Living Translation, copyright © 1996. Used by permission of Tyndale House Publishers, Inc., Wheaton, IL 60189. All rights reserved.

Scripture quotations marked NIV are from the Holy Bible, New International Version. Copyright © 1973, 1978, 1984, International Bible Society. Used by permission.

Scripture quotations marked KJV are from the King James Version of the Bible.

Scripture quotations marked THE MESSAGE are from *The Message: The Bible in Contemporary English,* copyright © 1993, 1994, 1995, 1996, 2000, 2001, 2002. Used by permission of NavPress Publishing Group.

Scripture quotations marked WEY are from the Weymouth Bible, *The New Testament in Modern Speech,* by Richard Francis Weymouth. Copyright © 1939 by James Clarke Co., publishers.

Cover design by Justin Evans
Design Director: Bill Johnson

Visit author's website: www.makeithappenlearninginstitute.com

Library of Congress Control Number: 2010940915
International Standard Book Number: 978-1-61638-440-1

First Edition

11 12 13 14 15 — 9 8 7 6 5 4 3 2 1
Printed in Canada

Contents

Author's Prayer

May the Lord empower all who read this book by the anointing of His Holy Spirit to be an overcoming servant leader who prevails with God in the business marketplace.

CB

And He [God] changes the times and the seasons; He removes kings and raises up kings; He gives wisdom to the wise And knowledge to those who have understanding.

—Daniel 2:21

A Make It Happen Dedication

This Make It Happen Book™ is dedicated to all of the godly leaders in business who every day fight the good fight of faith in the marketplace to honor God with their gifts and talents and bring Him glory by the way they represent Jesus Christ to the business community. As a business leader for many years, I have personally experienced the challenges and struggles that godly men and women face each day to practically live their faith and build the kingdom of God in the business world. I know first-hand that the marketplace environment can be a difficult and challenging place for people of faith to travel their faith journey; however, I also know that the marketplace is where the Lord is raising up kings in these last days to build His kingdom, glorify His holy name, and take the good news of the kingdom to the whole world. And the really cool thing about this chaordic frontier (the spiritual battleground where chaos meets order and good meets evil) is that kingdom ambassadors get to play an awesome part in this marketplace revival as the Lord changes the hearts of modern-day kings and revolutionizes the business world for His glory. All praise, glory, and honor to the King of kings and Lord of lords, forever and ever! Amen and amen!

The Make It Happen Team Values©

+ Make It Happen People Possess a Positive Make It Happen Attitude.

+ Make It Happen People Are Led by Servant Leaders.

+ Make It Happen People Are Service Enthusiasts.

+ Make It Happen People Take Calculated Risks in the Pursuit of Excellence.

+ Make It Happen People Work Extremely Hard and Have Lots of Fun.

+ Make It Happen People Invest and Participate in Training and Development.

+ Make It Happen People Celebrate Individual and Team Accomplishments with the Abundance Mentality.

+ Make It Happen People Foster a Safe Environment of Teamwork and Mutual Respect.

+ Make It Happen People Are Professionals.

Foreword

I WAS FIRST INTRODUCED to Gary Borgstede while attending a small group of local community business leaders five years ago. In short order, we became friends, and over the next few years I had the privilege of helping to coach Gary in the ways of the kingdom of God. At the time, Gary was vice president of finance at a very reputable hospital in our region. Over time, Gary began to share with me his fifteen-year journey in the healthcare industry. Because of my own experience and background working in a corporate environment before making the transition into full-time ministry, his story captivated my attention.

In *Kings Come Forth*, Gary addresses the delicate interfacing of the kingdom-minded business leader with the marketplace environment. He squarely and with scriptural precedent challenges business leaders to use their God-given positions to be change agents in their respective spheres of market influence. In our litigious world of exactness and political correctness, most Christian business leaders, out of fear, have a tendency to skirt the perimeter of their business environments and shy away from integrating real biblical standards and values. This is understandable. However, there is a real need for godly, Christian business people to rise to the occasion of desperate moral, character, and spiritual need in the world of business and facilitate change. As a pastor, I applaud those who are out on the highways and byways of the business world who are bold enough, with godly wisdom and a spiritually deft hand, to take a stand and entreat a spiritual climate change.

To affect this change, Gary explores the scriptural links between kings and priests and addresses the roles that each play and how they are to work together in advancing the kingdom. Gary addresses the frequently tentative nature of church leaders to properly understand and embrace the role the marketplace leader has and, as such, underutilize their God-given talents and marginalize them in their churches. Gary submits a challenge to church leaders to understand that God throughout Scripture placed kings and priests together for divine kingdom partnership. As a church leader who has been in ministry for more than twenty years, I have personally experienced the benefit of partnering with many wonderful, Christ-centered business leaders. I have had the opportunity to see the kingdom of God advanced and accelerated due to business leaders who realized their business acumen and talent were not just for their personal enrichment but, rather, for the advancement of the greatest cause on planet earth.

Gary Borgstede embodies the essence and balance of the corporate business leader and one who partners with the vision and mission of his local church with his time, talent, and treasure. Gary does not live in the world of concepts, ideas, and theories of being a king, but each day he lives it out as a servant-leader in his natural and spiritual families. Today, Gary serves on our church staff as the chief administrative officer and has the opportunity to serve his local church from within the organization. He is challenging us all to "make it happen!"

—RANDY CRAIGHEAD
EXECUTIVE PASTOR, CHURCH OF THE KING

Introduction

OR MORE THAN nineteen years, I have served the Lord as a king in His kingdom in the realm of business. As with many leaders of faith written about in the Bible, I have had my share of successes and failures on my personal faith journey. This book, *Kings Come Forth!*, is not about my successes nor my failures as a man of God in the Lord's kingdom; however, I am open and transparent regarding many aspects of my personal relationship with the Lord. In *The Maxwell Leadership Bible*, one of John Maxwell's leadership lessons includes this statement, "Without hope in the future, we lack power in the present."[1] With that in mind, I believe that the Lord has directed me to write *Kings Come Forth!* to inspire hope for the future and foster empowerment in the present for the many spirit-filled business leaders in God's kingdom on earth today.

The Holy Spirit has compelled me to write the message contained within the pages of this book as His message, not mine, from the perspective of a king in His kingdom. Through personal fellowship with the Lord, I believe it is His desire to awaken His anointed kings to their original purpose in the kingdom business through healthy kingdom partnership with His anointed priests. Since my educational background and professional experiences are entirely comprised in business, all supporting references to Scripture and biblical principles in the book are not the result of a formal Bible college education, but rather a real personal relationship with the actual Author of the Holy Scriptures, the Lord Jesus Christ Himself. Any personal revelation of the Scriptures is because of the Lord's faithfulness to fulfill the promise of His Word to personally lead His people into all truth and teach them all things through His Holy Spirit. For me, there is no greater fulfillment than that which comes from the leading and teaching of the Holy Spirit through my personal daily relationship with Jesus Christ, my Lord, Savior, and Friend.

In developing the literary style of the book, it is also very important to note that while I discriminately refer to godly business leaders throughout the entire book in the masculine form as kings, my purpose in doing so is nothing more than a matter of literary prose and contextual consistency and not a lack of respect for the many outstanding Spirit-filled female business leaders in the kingdom of God. In fact, I know full well that the business community is filled with many intelligent, competent, and influential business leaders who are outstanding women of faith committed to making a difference in life through their leadership. Therefore, for all of the female readers of *Kings Come Forth!*, please feel free to mentally substitute the context of the book from a masculine reference point of kings to a feminine reference point of queens since all of the material contained within these pages is completely gender neutral as well as kingdom applicable.

And lastly, as each reader begins to digest the message of *Kings Come Forth!* I pray that the Holy Spirit will fan into flame a renewed desire to become everything He created you to be as a Spirit-led business leader in His kingdom. To come forth in the power and might of the Holy Spirit and fulfill your

God-ordained kingdom assignment as a king in God's kingdom can be one of the most rewarding aspects of your personal faith journey with the Lord. I look forward to taking this faith journey with you to build God's kingdom in every sphere of influence, especially the sphere of the modern-day business world.

1

The Great Distinction of Kings

> Yours, O LORD, is the greatness, the power, the
> glory, the victory, and the majesty. Everything in
> the heavens and on earth is yours, O LORD, and
> this is your kingdom. We adore you as the one
> who is over all things. Wealth and honor come
> from you alone, for you rule over everything. Power
> and might are in your hand, and at your discre-
> tion people are made great and given strength.
> —*1 Chronicles 29:11–12, NLT*

KINGS THAT TROUBLE OR OPPRESS

The very first king that we see in the Bible is the Pharaoh of Egypt during the time of Abram. Furthermore, the first time that the people of God encounter an official king with authority over them, it is once again, the Pharaoh of Egypt. Unfortunately, the title, Pharaoh of Egypt, means "king that troubles or oppresses."[1] For four hundred years the Israelites lived in Egyptian bondage to the Pharaoh and were subject to the curse of his ruthless oppression of their gifts and talents for his own purposes.

To state the obvious, the slavery of God's people to build a kingdom of oppression under the authority of an oppressive ruler was never God's original intent or purpose for His people. To the contrary, God's desire and original intent for His people has been and always will be to rule and reign with Him on earth and in heaven, now, and forever more. In Genesis 1:28, the Word of God states, "Then God blessed them, and God said to them, 'Be fruitful and multiply; fill the earth and subdue it; have dominion over the fish of the sea, over the birds of the air, and over every living thing that moves on the earth.'" From this passage it is clear that from the beginning God never intended for His people to be in bondage to an oppressive ruler of any kind but rather to rule and reign on the earth in His blessing.

KINGS THAT PREVAIL WITH GOD

In stark contrast to the Pharaoh of Egypt, the very first official king that we see in the Bible with legitimate authority over God's people is King Saul, the king of Israel anointed by God to lead His people in a land of freedom and blessing. It is important to note that the title, King of Israel, means "king that prevails with God."[2]

The distinction between a king that troubles or oppresses and a king that prevails with God is an important distinction because modern-day kings in the marketplace—business leaders—whether they know it or not, are leading with a prevalent tendency toward one or the other of these two distinctly different leadership expressions. The business leader who leads as a king that troubles or oppresses leads with a spirit of taskmaster and possesses defining taskmaster leadership character traits. And likewise, the business leader who leads as a king that prevails with God leads with a spirit of servant leadership and possesses defining servant leadership character traits. In the pages ahead I will illustrate the pertinent differences in taskmaster leadership and servant leadership by specifically identifying the character traits of each leadership expression as well as providing a biblical illustration of each type of leader from the Word of God.

The business leader who leads as a king that troubles or

oppresses is a proud arrogant leader with a selfish heart and possesses the following taskmaster leadership character traits to a certain degree:

TASKMASTER LEADERSHIP CHARACTER TRAITS

+ Internal motivation driven by power

+ Ego-centric perspective focused on self

+ Decisions grounded in fear and insecurity

+ Tasks people without the proper tools and resources

+ Takes from people more than gives to them

+ Recognizes self accomplishments at the expense of others

+ Tears people down physically, spiritually, and emotionally

The biblical account in Exodus 1:8–14 provides an excellent picture of a classic taskmaster leader that troubles or oppresses:

> Now there arose a new king over Egypt, who did not know Joseph. And he said to his people, "Look, the people of the children of Israel are more and mightier than we [internal motivation driven by power]; come, let us deal shrewdly with them [egocentric perspective focused on self], lest they multiply, and it happen, in the event of war, that they also join our enemies and fight against us [decisions grounded in fear and insecurity], and so go up out of the land." Therefore they set taskmasters over them to afflict them with their burdens [tasks people without the proper tools and

resources]. And they built for Pharaoh supply cities, Pithom and Raamses [recognizes self accomplishments at the expense of others]. But the more they afflicted them, the more they multiplied and grew. And they were in dread of the children of Israel. So the Egyptians made the children of Israel serve with rigor. And they made their lives bitter with hard bondage—in mortar, in brick, and in all manner of service in the field [takes from people more than gives]. All their service in which they made them serve was with rigor [tears people down physically, spiritually, and emotionally].

On the other hand, the business leader who leads as a king that prevails with God is a humble, confident leader with an unselfish heart and possesses the following servant leadership character traits to a certain degree:

SERVANT LEADERSHIP CHARACTER TRAITS

- Internal motivation driven by influence
- People-centric perspective focused on others
- Decisions grounded in faith and security
- Equips people with the proper tools and resources
- Gives to people more than takes from them
- Recognizes the accomplishments of others at the expense of self
- Builds people up physically, spiritually, and emotionally

The biblical account in the Book of Nehemiah provides an excellent picture of a classic servant leader that prevails with God.

It came to pass in the month of Chislev, in the twentieth year, as I [Nehemiah] was in Shushan the citadel, that Hanani one of my brethren came with men from Judah; and I asked them concerning the Jews who had escaped, who had survived the captivity, and concerning Jerusalem. And they said to me, "The survivors who are left from the captivity in the province are there in great distress and reproach. The wall of Jerusalem is also broken down, and its gates are burned with fire." So it was, when I heard these words, that I sat down and wept, and mourned for many days; I was fasting and praying before the God of heaven [people-centric perspective focused on others].

—NEHEMIAH 1:1–4

Then the king said to me [Nehemiah], "What do you request?" So I prayed to the God of heaven. And I said to the king, "If it pleases the king, and if your servant has found favor in your sight, I ask that you send me to Judah, to the city of my fathers' tombs, that I may rebuild it." Then the king said to me (the queen also sitting beside him), "How long will your journey be? And when will you return?" So it pleased the king to send me; and I set him a time. Furthermore I said to the king, "If it pleases the king, let letters be given to me for the governors of the region beyond the River, that they must permit me to pass through till I come to Judah, and a letter to Asaph the keeper of the king's forest, that he must give me timber to make beams for the gates of the citadel which pertains to the temple, for the city wall, and for the house that I will occupy." And the king granted them to me according to the good hand of my God upon me [internal motivation driven by influence].

—NEHEMIAH 2:4–8

Then Judah said, "The strength of the laborers is failing, and there is so much rubbish that we are not able to build the wall." And our adversaries said, "They will neither know nor see anything, till we come into their midst and kill them and cause the work to cease." So it was, when the Jews who dwelt near them came, that they told us ten times, "From whatever place you turn, they will be upon us." Therefore I [Nehemiah] positioned men behind the lower parts of the wall, at the openings; and I set the people according to their families, with their swords, their spears, and their bows [equips people with the proper tools and resources]. And I looked, and arose and said to the nobles, to the leaders, and to the rest of the people, "Do not be afraid of them. Remember the Lord, great and awesome, and fight for your brethren, your sons, your daughters, your wives, and your houses [decisions grounded in faith and security]."

—NEHEMIAH 4:10–14

Moreover, from the time that I [Nehemiah] was appointed to be their governor in the land of Judah, from the twentieth year until the thirty-second year of King Artaxerxes, twelve years, neither I nor my brothers ate the governor's provisions. But the former governors who were before me laid burdens on the people, and took from them bread and wine, besides forty shekels of silver. Yes, even their servants bore rule over the people, but I did not do so, because of the fear of God. Indeed, I also continued the work on this wall, and we did not buy any land. All my servants were gathered there for the work. And at my table were one hundred and fifty Jews and rulers, besides those who came to us from the nations around us. Now that which was prepared daily was one ox and six choice sheep. Also fowl were prepared for me, and once every ten days an abundance of all kinds of wine. Yet in spite of this I did not demand the governor's provisions, because the bondage was heavy on this people. Remember me, my God, for good, according to all that I have done for this people [gives to people more than takes from them].

—NEHEMIAH 5:14–19

Then it was, when the wall was built and I had hung the doors, when the gatekeepers, the singers, and the Levites had been appointed, that I gave the charge of Jerusalem to my brother Hanani, and Hananiah the leader of the citadel, for he was a faithful man and feared God more than many [recognizes the accomplishments of others at the expense of self].

—NEHEMIAH 7:1

Now at the dedication of the wall of Jerusalem they sought out the Levites in all their places, to bring them to Jerusalem to celebrate the dedication with gladness, both with thanksgivings and singing, with cymbals and stringed instruments and harps [builds people up physically, spiritually, and emotionally].

—NEHEMIAH 12:27

From these two very different biblical accounts of leadership, the spirit of taskmaster and the spirit of servant leadership are clearly identified and exposed for our learning, benefit, and practical application as business leaders in the current-day marketplace. And if the examples of Pharaoh and Nehemiah don't make it clear enough that servant leadership is the superior leadership practice, the Lord Himself clarifies it for us. In Matthew 23:11–12, He states:

> But he who is greatest among you shall be your servant. And whoever exalts himself will be humbled, and he who humbles himself will be exalted.

The humble servant leader is the leader that God can use mightily in His kingdom business.

A KING'S LEGITIMATE CALLING BY GOD

For God to mightily use a business leader as a vessel of honor in His kingdom, a business leader must be legitimately called by God to lead as a king in the kingdom. Since the Word of God says in Acts 10:34 (WEY), "God makes no distinctions between one man and another," we can believe that He also doesn't make any distinctions between one business leader and another that He legitimately calls and appoints to lead in His kingdom. However, this should not be confused with the different gifts and talents that God does indeed give to different leaders in their respective leadership roles in the kingdom. The point I am clarifying is that God is no respecter of persons when it comes to His calling, but He does in fact give different gifts and talents to people for His use in the kingdom.

From the biblical account found in 1 Samuel 9:15–19 regarding the calling of King Saul, the very first commander-in-chief of God's people, we can learn seven significant spiritual principles that apply to every business leader's calling in God:

> Now the LORD had told Samuel [the prophet of God] in his ear the day before Saul came, saying, "Tomorrow about this time I will send you a man [sent by God]

from the land of Benjamin [belongs to the family of God], and you shall anoint him commander over My people Israel [ANOINTED BY GOD TO LEAD], that he may save My people from the hand of the Philistines [assigned purpose from God]; for I have looked upon My people, because their cry has come to Me." So when Samuel saw Saul, the LORD said to him, "There he is, the man of whom I spoke to you. This one shall reign over My people." Then Saul drew near to Samuel in the gate, [seeks godly relationships] and said, "Please tell me, where is the seer's house?" Samuel answered Saul and said, "I am the seer. Go up before me to the high place, for you shall eat with me today; and tomorrow I will let you go [destiny is released through godly relationships] and will tell you all that is in your heart [open to the Word of God]."

SEVEN SPIRITUAL PRINCIPLES RELEVANT FOR EVERY GODLY BUSINESS LEADER

1. A godly business leader is sent by God.

2. A godly business leader belongs to the family of God.

3. A godly business leader is anointed by God to lead.

4. A godly business leader has an assigned purpose from God.

5. A godly business leader seeks godly relationships.

6. A godly business leader has a destiny released through godly relationships.

7. A godly business leader has a heart open to the
Word of God.

A godly business leader is sent by God.

So let's look at the first spiritual principle relevant to current-
day godly business leaders. What does it mean to be sent by
God as a business leader in the marketplace? I believe it is by no
accident that business leaders find themselves leading in business. That's simply because God is our Creator and He knows
every hair on our head—He does nothing in our lives by accident. In Matthew 10:29–31, the Word of God states:

> Are not two sparrows sold for a copper coin? And not
> one of them falls to the ground apart from your Father's
> will. But the very hairs of your head are all numbered.
> Do not fear therefore; you are of more value than many
> sparrows.

Therefore, if God cares so much about even the sparrows
such that none of them fall to the ground outside of His will,
how much more should we believe that He cares about us and
His will for our lives? As the omniscient (all knowing) heavenly Father, God knows everything about our lives, including
the vocation that He specifically made for each one of us. So, if
you enjoy leading in business, exercising your gifts and talents
in the marketplace to make a difference in the lives of others,
you can rest assured that God has purposefully sent you to the
marketplace as a business leader—it's not by accident!

A godly business leader belongs to the family of God.

Secondly, godly business leaders belong to the family of God.
Now if you're not 100 percent certain at this moment whether
or not you are legitimately part of God's family, then we can

easily take care of that with a simple prayer of faith. However, before I share the prayer of faith with you, I think it is important that you understand our godly heritage of faith. In Genesis 17:1–7, the Word of God says:

> When Abram was ninety-nine years old, the Lord appeared to Abram and said to him, "I am Almighty God; walk before Me and be blameless. And I will make My covenant between Me and you, and will multiply you exceedingly." Then Abram fell on his face, and God talked with him, saying: "As for Me, behold, My covenant is with you, and you shall be a father of many nations. No longer shall your name be called Abram, but your name shall be Abraham; for I have made you a father of many nations. I will make you exceedingly fruitful; and I will make nations of you, and *kings shall come from you*. And I will establish My covenant between Me and you and your descendants after you in their generations, for an everlasting covenant, to be God to you and your descendants after you."

At this point, you might be asking what does the story of Abraham have to do with my being part of the family of God. Well, it has everything to do with it because in order to become part of the family of God, you must have the same kind of faith in God that Abraham had as the father of our faith. In fact, Galatians 3:6–7 (KJV) says:

> Even as Abraham believed God, and it was accounted to him for righteousness. Know ye therefore that they which are of faith, the same are the children of Abraham.

Based on these verses, faith is clearly established as a key characteristic of the family of God. And to be even more direct, it is only by faith—believing God like Abraham—that you and I can be born into the family of God.

However, it is also very important for us to understand that faith in God alone does not make us legitimate children of the living God. In fact, the Word of God states in James 2:20 that "even the demons believe [in God]—and tremble!" This statement makes it clear that just believing in God doesn't make us legitimate members of His family. Well then, what does? Have you ever heard the saying that "blood is thicker than water," meaning that blood relatives carry a deeper relationship? Well, it's actually the same way in the family of God.

You see, while God is our heavenly Father who created each one of us, your sin and my sin causes us to fall short of His glory as well as separates us from Him. And it really doesn't matter who we are or how good we think we are. Sin is sin and it separates me and you from God. The Word of God states in Romans 3:23 that "all have sinned and fall short of the glory of God." And furthermore, the Word of God soberly states in Romans 6:23 that "the wages of sin is death." As you can imagine, this is not good! Because God is a righteous judge, His justice demands payment for our sin. Unfortunately, there is no way around the death penalty for the consequences of our sin. This means that your sin debt and mine will eternally separate us from God unless the debt is paid. This is where the good news begins!

Because God is also an unconditionally loving Father, He did something extraordinary for you and me so that we wouldn't have to pay the death penalty for our sin. The Word of God states in John 3:16 that "God so loved the world that He gave His only begotten Son, that whoever believes in Him should not perish but have everlasting life." In a totally outrageous act of love, God chose to pay the wages of our sin with the blood of His own dearly beloved Son, Jesus Christ. In Romans 5:8–9, the Word of God clearly states that "God demonstrates His own love toward us, in that while we were still sinners, Christ died for us. Much more then, having now been justified by His blood, we shall be saved from wrath through Him." Now do you see what I mean when I say that "blood is thicker than water" in the family of God? It is the shed blood of Jesus that totally sets us free from sin and death and makes the difference in our eternal relationship with God.

With all of that said, if you want to be born into the family of God with right standing as a legitimate, blood-bought, child of the living God, all you have to do is believe and pray a simple prayer of faith in brokenness and repentance to the Lord Jesus Christ. The Bible states in Romans 10:9–10 "that if you confess with your mouth the Lord Jesus and believe in your heart that God has raised Him from the dead, you will be saved. For with the heart one believes unto righteousness, and with the mouth confession is made unto salvation." Therefore, it is vitally important that you read and pray out loud the following simple prayer to Jesus if you desire to be saved by His grace through faith.

A Simple Prayer of Faith

Dear Lord Jesus,

I confess to You that I am a sinner in need of Your forgiveness. I thank You for dying on the cross for me and shedding Your blood as payment for the penalty of my sin. In faith, I repent and turn from my sin, believing that You died and rose from the dead so that I will not perish, but have everlasting life with You as my Lord and Savior. With thanksgiving in my heart, I receive the

*free gift of new life in You forevermore. All praise, glory,
and honor be to You, forever and ever! In Jesus name I
pray. Amen and amen!*

Signature: _____

Date: _____

CB

My friend, if you have just prayed this simple prayer of faith,
then you are now born into the family of God as a new creation
in Christ. In fact, 2 Corinthians 5:17–18 states the good news,
"If anyone is in Christ, he is a new creation; old things have
passed away; behold, all things have become new." Therefore, let
me be the first to welcome you into the family of God and your
new life in Christ. I encourage you to find a good Bible-believing
church in your community where you can find other believers in
Christ and begin learning how to do kingdom life with them as
a disciple of the Lord. As you will soon discover, kingdom life is
a journey never meant for us to do alone.

And let me tell you some even more good news! As a child
of God through faith in Jesus, you have been born into royalty
as a joint heir with Christ to the kingdom of God. Is it too hard
to believe? Well then let the Word of God settle it for you.
In Romans 8:16–17, the Word of God says that "The Spirit
Himself bears witness with our spirit that we are children of
God, and if children, then heirs—heirs of God and joint heirs
with Christ, if indeed we suffer with Him, that we may also be
glorified together." Wow! There you have it, the truth of God
affirming that we are heirs of God and joint heirs with Jesus.
This means that you and I are royalty in the kingdom of God

fulfilling God's promise to Abraham in Genesis 17:6 that kings would in fact come from him. Praise be to God!

A godly business leader is anointed by God to lead.

Webster's Dictionary defines *anointed* as: "consecrated [set apart or dedicated for a sacred use.]"[3] Therefore, to be a leader anointed by God is to be set apart by God for His noble use as a leader in His kingdom and believe it or not, His kingdom reaches into every sphere of influence, including the marketplace.

Ed Silvoso writes in his book, *Anointed for Business*, what it feels like to be anointed for business: "I thoroughly enjoyed dealing, buying, selling, and hiring. The pressure was always on, but each time it approached the boiling point, I reached for what I called the Jesus chair. This was a chair I had purposely placed in my office. When things became unmanageable, I would close the door, kneel by the chair and ask for divine guidance. Repeatedly God provided it. Sometimes He did it in a quiet way. At other times He gave me specific directions. More than once He performed business miracles in answer to those prayers. It was so reassuring to know that Jesus was there and that He anointed me for the job I had."[4]

As a business leader in the marketplace, God wants you to be reassured that He is there with you and that He has anointed you for the job you have. In fact, one of the names of God is Jehovah Shammah, The Lord Is There, which means that wherever you go, the Lord is already there available to assist you whenever you call upon Him.[5] As you and I both know, the marketplace can be a treacherous place for the man or woman of God seeking to do His will; however, we have no reason to fear because the Lord promises to be there with us in every situation. In 2 Chronicles 16:9, the Word of God says that "the eyes of the LORD run to and fro throughout the whole earth, to show Himself strong

15

on behalf of those whose heart is loyal to Him." This promise from God is good news for anyone in the marketplace whose heart is loyal to God because no matter what situation you may encounter, God has promised to have your back. Furthermore, God sweetens His promise by stating in Romans 8:31, "If God is for us, who can be against us?" Simply put, God is for us, my friend, and He has specifically anointed us to be His kingdom ambassadors in the marketplace.

A godly business leader has an assigned purpose from God.

As God's kingdom ambassadors to the marketplace, you and I each have a unique and specifically assigned purpose from God that will help build His kingdom on earth. Jesse Duplantis states in his book, *The Everyday Visionary*, that the kingdom of God is a method of doing things God's way.[6] Therefore, regardless of what God has called each of us to distinctly do for Him on earth in building His kingdom and fulfilling the plans that He has for us in the marketplace, we must all learn to do things His way. And when we do, He gives us a future and a hope as stated in Jeremiah 29:11–12 (NLT), "'For I know the plans I have for you,' says the LORD. 'They are plans for good and not for disaster, to give you a future and a hope.'"

It doesn't matter the profession—plumber, accountant, hair stylist, contractor, doctor, nurse, bus driver, or any other profession—we are all created by God with value and purpose in the kingdom of God. Ephesians 2:10 states, "We are His workmanship, created in Christ Jesus for good works, which God prepared beforehand that we should walk in them." It doesn't get any plainer than that. We are God's workmanship created for good works. But it's up to you and me whether or not we will choose to walk in them and fulfill our assigned purpose.

Now if you're thinking that you really don't know your

assigned purpose from God, let me share with you a wisdom principle that I learned from Dr. Mike Murdock about discovering your God ordained purpose. Dr. Murdock teaches that the problem which infuriates you the most can actually be the problem that God intends for you to help solve.[7] As you ponder this wisdom principle, be attentive in your spirit to those things that tend to upset you the most because they could just be a clue to the specific assignment that God wants you to help solve as His kingdom ambassador on the earth.

An example of this from the Bible can be seen in the call of God on Moses to be a deliverer of the Israelites from the oppression of Pharaoh. The actual biblical account of this example is recorded in Exodus 2:11–15. When Moses witnessed an Egyptian taskmaster beating one of his fellow Israelites, he became enraged by the injustice. Unfortunately, though, Moses took matters into his own hands and actually killed the Egyptian taskmaster, which was not the way God intended for Moses to deliver His people. As a result, Moses had to flee into the desert for forty years until God developed the character necessary for Moses to return to Egypt in the power of God's might and deliver the Israelites from the hand of Pharaoh in the manner that God intended. Moses' call never changed from that day he became enraged and killed an Egyptian taskmaster; however, the character of Moses most definitely did change as God prepared him in the desert to fulfill his God ordained purpose on earth to be a deliverer of the Israelite people.

A godly business leader seeks godly relationships.

I've heard it said that in life, there are very few successful lone rangers—why even the Lone Ranger had Tonto. You see, the point is that to do life successfully, everyone needs someone who will stand by their side and be a real friend to them in the good times and even the bad times. This truth is found in Proverbs 17:17 which states that "A friend loves at all times, and a brother is born for adversity."

As a godly leader in the marketplace, I know all too well how lonely it can sometimes be to stand in the gap for righteousness, loving your enemies, blessing those that curse you, and giving until it hurts. Without other godly people to do life with me, speak life over me, believe in me the way that God believes in me, and love me enough to tell me the truth even when it hurts, I seriously shudder to think about what kind of leader and person I could easily become. I thank God every day for the wonderful spiritual family that He has supernaturally chosen for me and my family.

From my own personal experiences, I intimately know the pain and misery created for myself and others resulting from poor personal choices made in an environment of separation, isolation, and loneliness away from the family of God. Having been at the bottom of the pit of life with nothing but myself and the results of my poor personal choices, trust me when I say that I don't ever want to be in that situation again. Because the Lord of my salvation is a strong tower and a very present help in time of need, He delivered me from the hand of the enemy to my soul. Because God has a tremendous destiny for me, I now realize that the devil was working double time to take me out, destroy my family, and steal my destiny in God.

I don't know if you know it or not, but the devil has a mission statement in the Word of God directed at you and me. In John 10:10 the Word states that "the thief [satan] does not come except to steal, and to kill, and to destroy." This means that the devil hates God so much that his greatest desire is to steal, kill, and destroy that which God loves the most—and that is you and me! The most effective way that satan can steal, kill, and destroy people is by separating them from the family of God, isolating them into a life of loneliness, and then going in for the kill. When we are isolated and separated from the body of Christ, we become easy prey for satan to kill our entire destiny: physically, mentally, socially, financially, and—the most deadly killing of all—spiritually. But thank God that the Lord Jesus Christ also has a mission statement found in the Word of God. In the same verse of John 10:10, the Word says, "I [Jesus] have come that they may have life, and that they may have it more abundantly." Praise God for His ultimate promise of life and life more abundantly for all believers in Him!

Another reason why it is so important for believers in the marketplace to seek godly relationships with other believers is because God created us to not only need Him, but to also need each other. Even the cross illustrates this principle with a vertical beam reaching up to heaven signifying our dependence on God and a horizontal beam reaching out side-to-side signifying our dependence on one another.

The wisest man who ever lived, King Solomon, states in Proverbs 24:5–6, "A wise man is strong, Yes, a man of knowledge increases strength; For by wise counsel you will wage your own war, And in a multitude of counselors there is safety." Without doubt, godly business leaders find strength, knowledge, wise counsel, and safety when we seek relationships with other godly business leaders and commit to do life with them as a real friend in God. Trust me, the Lord cares deeply about our relationships in the family of God; so much so that I believe He personally chooses our spiritual family in the kingdom of God.

In fact, by a divine miracle appointment in my own life, the Lord supernaturally directed my steps to my spiritual family at

Church of the King in Mandeville, Louisiana. It's a long story, but my wife and I were actually attending two different churches for a time. She was attending a new church in our community led by an anointed senior pastor named Steve Robinson whom she had heard on a local Christian radio station. I was attending a new satellite church in our community of the home church where I was saved many years prior. While attending church each week, my wife developed a relationship with one of Pastor Steve's long-time faithful friends—an authentic woman of God who began to very effectively disciple her. Through the process, they were praying that I would accept an invitation from Pastor Steve to personally meet with him; however, I was not free in my conscience to accept his open offer and declined it many times. So my wife just kept telling me that Pastor Steve was praying for me and that he would be glad to meet with me anytime. With Pastor Steve's open invitation, my wife continued to believe that God would somehow find a way for me and Pastor Steve to meet with one another.

Well, months had gone by and we were still attending different churches when Christmas came around. So my wife asked me if I would please go to church with her and the family on Christmas Eve to celebrate Christmas together as a family. Of course I agreed. It was at that one and only service where I saw Pastor Steve for the first time and learned a little bit about him including what he looked like. If not for that service, I wouldn't have known Pastor Steve if he was standing next to me because I had never seen him before in my life. After that service, my wife and I resumed our attendance at our two separate churches—the one she called home and the one I had called home for many years. But little did I know that God had a new home in mind for me.

One weekend a couple of months after that Christmas Eve service, my wife's friend invited her to attend a women's weekend retreat with her and Pastor Steve's wife. As a result, I was left with my five kids for the weekend for the very first time. Not knowing what I should do with them on that Saturday morning, I decided that I would take them to the park and let them play while I reflected upon the condition of my life. I was feeling alone, confused, and desperate for the right changes in my life, but couldn't seem to find a way out of the pit that surrounded me.

But then, as I was standing in the park, I looked over to my right and saw Pastor Steve playing with his kids not more than ten feet away from me. At first I was shocked to see him standing there, but then the Lord spoke to me in a small, soft, but firm voice, and said, "You better go talk to him. I put him here just for you to meet him." With a reverence for the Lord, I stepped out of my comfort zone and went over to introduce myself. "Excuse me, are you Pastor Steve? You don't really know me, but my name is Gary Borgstede. My wife is actually on the weekend retreat with your wife and has in fact driven over there with her in the same car. So I thought I should come over and introduce myself."

After thinking for a moment, in total surprise, Pastor Steve responded, "Wait a minute, you're the 'Ochsner' guy! I've been praying for you. What are you doing here? Have you had lunch yet? Would you like to join me and the kids to get something to eat?" With a little uneasiness, I accepted his invitation immediately knowing that he must be a mighty man of God if he was brave enough to go to lunch with me and a combined total of eight kids between his three and my five. What a sight we must have been, having lunch together with eight kids in a country club restaurant. Anyhow, while driving in separate cars to the country club, Pastor Steve excitedly called his wife to let her know about the miracle encounter in the park as well as our lunch appointment together. As you can imagine, my wife and her friends were utterly amazed at the awesomeness of God when Pastor Steve's wife told them what God was doing with him and me.

I often thank God for personally inviting me into a relationship with Pastor Steve as my senior pastor whom I greatly respect and dearly love as a mighty man of God. Additionally, I am grateful to God for personally choosing my new church home and at the same time restoring me as the spiritual head of my family as a long-term result of this miracle encounter with Pastor Steve in the park. I am so amazed at the faithfulness of God to complete the good work that He begins in us and to work all things together for good to those who love Him and are called according to His purpose.

By my own personal testimony, I know that God cares as much about your spiritual family as He cares about mine. I know that He will go to great lengths to direct your steps to the right spiritual family in the family of God; therefore, be open to the leading of the Holy Spirit and expect Him to setup special divine appointments that will fulfill the good plan of God for you and your family.

A godly business leader has a destiny released through godly relationships.

In Proverbs 13:20, the Word of God states, "He who walks with wise men will be wise, But the companion of fools will be destroyed"; therefore, we can conclude from the wisdom of God that if a godly business leader wants to see his God-given destiny and legacy completely fulfilled in God, it is vitally important that he or she seek and find a small group of wise, godly counselors to faithfully do life with them on a consistent daily, weekly, and annual basis. To do otherwise could indeed have tragic consequences to a business leader's destiny and legacy as can be learned from the history of the life of King Rehoboam, the son of King Solomon.

Unfortunately, in the history of Israel, because of poor personal choices and weak leadership character, not all of the kings of Israel fulfilled their destiny and legacy to be kings that prevailed with God. One such king of Israel who failed to fulfill his God-ordained destiny to reign over the entire nation of Israel is King Rehoboam. Instead of being remembered in history as the king of Israel who successfully succeeded his father, King Solomon, in building the nation of Israel, King Rehoboam is instead remembered in the pages of history as the king that split the nation of Israel because he rejected the wisdom of his father's elder council.

In the Bible, 2 Chronicles 10:1–19 records the tragic consequences of King Rehoboam's rejection of wise godly counsel and the resulting historic split of the nation of Israel into two kingdoms.

> And Rehoboam went to Shechem, for all Israel had gone to Shechem to make him king. So it happened, when Jeroboam the son of Nebat heard it (he was in Egypt, where he had fled from the presence of King Solomon), that Jeroboam returned from Egypt. Then they sent for him and called him. And Jeroboam and all Israel came and spoke to Rehoboam, saying, "Your father made our yoke heavy; now therefore, lighten the burdensome service of your father and his heavy yoke which he put on us, and we will serve you." So he said to them, "Come back to me after three days." And the people departed. Then King Rehoboam consulted the

elders who stood before his father Solomon while he still lived, saying, "How do you advise me to answer these people?" And they spoke to him, saying, "If you are kind to these people, and please them, and speak good words to them, they will be your servants forever." But he rejected the advice which the elders had given him, and consulted the young men who had grown up with him, who stood before him. And he said to them, "What advice do you give? How should we answer this people who have spoken to me, saying, 'Lighten the yoke which your father put on us'?" Then the young men who had grown up with him spoke to him, saying, "Thus you should speak to the people who have spoken to you, saying, 'Your father made our yoke heavy, but you make it lighter on us'—thus you shall say to them: 'My little finger shall be thicker than my father's waist! And now, whereas my father put a heavy yoke on you, I will add to your yoke; my father chastised you with whips, but I will chastise you with scourges!'" So Jeroboam and all the people came to Rehoboam on the third day, as the king had directed, saying, "Come back to me the third day." Then the king answered them roughly. King Rehoboam rejected the advice of the elders, and he spoke to them according to the advice of the young men, saying, "My father made your yoke heavy, but I will add to it; my father chastised you with whips, but I will chastise you with scourges!" So the king did not listen to the people; for the turn of events was from God, that the Lord might fulfill His word, which He had spoken by the hand of Ahijah the Shilonite to Jeroboam the son of Nebat. Now when all Israel saw that the king did not listen to them, the people answered the king, saying: "What share have we in David? We have no inheritance in the son of Jesse. Every man to your tents, O Israel! Now see to your own house, O David!"

So all Israel departed to their tents. But Rehoboam reigned over the children of Israel who dwelt in the cities of Judah. Then King Rehoboam sent Hadoram, who was in charge of revenue; but the children of Israel stoned him with stones, and he died. Therefore King Rehoboam mounted his chariot in haste to flee to Jerusalem. So Israel has been in rebellion against the house of David to this day [with the kingdom split in two].

Because the Word of God emphasizes the fact that King Rehoboam rejected the advice of the elders by recording it twice in the same story of Scripture, it is imperative that godly business leaders in the marketplace take special heed to learn from his insolent leadership mistake. If King Rehoboam, the son of King Solomon, the wisest man who ever lived, can make such a big mistake, why should we be so bold as to think that we could be immune from making the same kind of tragic mistake? The only way to potentially inoculate ourselves from making this kind of mistake is to diligently seek, invite, and welcome godly advice and counsel into our lives. Great leaders are extremely effective because they listen well to the advice and guidance of wise godly counsel.

According to Bible wisdom, a real friend is someone whom is willing to risk your approval and tell you truth that will help you learn, grow, and develop into the person that God has created you to be. Proverbs 27:17 (NIV) states, "As iron sharpens iron, so does one man sharpen another." This means that as real friends do life together, they will sharpen one another with truth spoken in love. And as we all know, sometimes the truth about ourselves can hurt; however, if we stay open to receiving truth into our lives and remain teachable in spirit, our character will flourish and grow through the process. Much like a plant pruned in the spring time of its dead, life-sucking branches so that it can flourish with new life-producing buds, we too must have people willing to help prune the dead things in our lives so that we can grow and flourish in God. Hebrews 12:11 speaks of the pruning process of God through chastening by stating, "Now no chastening seems to be joyful for the present, but painful; nevertheless, afterward it yields the peaceable fruit of righteousness to those who have been trained by it." Therefore, as we embrace the pruning shears of life through the chastening truth of God's Word, we can trust God that our lives will begin to flourish in even new and greater ways. Praise God for the flourishing life found in Him and the truth of His Word!

A godly business leader has a heart open to the Word of God.

Because marketplace leaders are geared for action, it is important that they be fully grounded in the Word of God to ensure that they become effective leaders "in" the world and not effective leaders "of" the world. Although subtle, there is a huge difference that godly business leaders must possess as kingdom ambassadors of the Most High God in the marketplace. I believe that the major distinction of being an effective leader in the world versus an effective leader of the world is where our faith and strength come from.

Godly business leaders effective "in" the world receive their strength from having faith in God to help them get the job done; whereas, business leaders "of" the world receive their strength from having faith in themselves only to get the job done, which by the way is a faulty strength—it can easily fail when tested under stress and pressure. On the other hand, authentic strength received from the Spirit of God living on the inside of a godly believer becomes even stronger when tested under stress and pressure. My senior pastor likes to illustrate this point in his teachings with the two following questions and answers. "What do you get when you squeeze oranges? Orange juice, right? Well then, what do you get when you squeeze Christians? Christ-likeness!" This simply means that when believers are tested through the trials and tribulations of this world, they don't get bitter; they just get better, as the character of Christ is developed in them through each test and trial of life.

The apostle John specifically elaborates on the distinction of being "in" the world versus "of" the world in 1 John 4:4–6, stating:

> You are of God, little children, and have overcome them, because He who is in you is greater than he who is in the world. They are of the world. Therefore they speak as of the world, and the world hears them. We are of God. He who knows God hears us; he who is not of God does not hear us. By this we know the spirit of truth and the spirit of error.

According to the apostle John, we have strength to overcome the world even though we are in it because the Spirit of the living God in us is greater than the spirit of antichrist living in the world. I know this may be heavy; however, a godly business leader must know the difference and demonstrate it by the power of the Holy Spirit living and working in him as he effectively leads and walks by faith in the marketplace.

I've heard it said, "faith is Forward Action Inspired Through Him." This statement helps define the kind of action-oriented faith that godly business leaders must possess to be an effective leader "in" the marketplace rather than an effective leader "of" the marketplace. And the Bible says that this kind of faith actually comes by hearing the Word of God. By the way, do you know how doubt, the opposite of faith, comes? It also comes by hearing, but instead of hearing by the faith-inspiring words from the Word of God, doubt comes by hearing the faithless words from the negative dimensions of worldly culture around us. Romans 10:17 (KJV) is clear, "Faith cometh by hearing, and hearing by the word of God"; therefore, godly business leaders must become rooted in the Word of God to be faith-filled effective leaders "in" the world, but not "of" the world.

If perhaps you're challenged by this responsibility as a godly business leader, then let the example of Joshua be an encouragement to you. The Bible says in Joshua 1:8, "This Book of the Law shall not depart from your mouth, but you shall meditate in it day and night, that you may observe to do according to all that is written in it. For then you will make your way prosperous, and then you will have good success." This verse offers us a wonderful promise from God—if you and I make the Word of God a priority in our life and do what it says to do, we can expect God to help us to make our way prosperous and have good success, despite the trials and tribulations of life that we may face along the way. Amen!

THE DEAD SEA REVELATION

Because the Lord Himself emphasized and demonstrated the significant distinction between leaders of the world and leaders in the kingdom, it wouldn't be fitting for me to end this chapter without closing on the importance of dying to self in becoming a genuine servant leader in the kingdom of God. Mark 10:42–45 tells us:

> Jesus called them to Himself and said to them, "You know that those who are considered rulers over the Gentiles lord it over them, and their great ones exercise authority over them. Yet it shall not be so among you; but whoever desires to become great among you shall

be your servant. And whoever of you desires to be first shall be slave of all. For even the Son of Man did not come to be served, but to serve, and to give His life a ransom for many."

So then the question becomes, how do we practically become a servant to others in the realm of the marketplace? And the answer is the same way Jesus did—by dying to self. Let me explain further with the revelation of the Dead Sea that I received one Christmas season when God revealed to me something very special about the Dead Sea.

During this particular Christmas season, I was teaching about the Dead Sea to the men in my small group. I shared with them that the Dead Sea is dead because it receives a river inflow, but has no river outflow, which causes it to stagnate and die. Therefore, I was explaining how important it is for us to be people that not only receive from others, but also give out to others. In so doing, we would be like a growing flourishing river of life and blessing rather than a dead and stagnant sea.

Because this fact of the Dead Sea had always been a powerful illustration to me of the spiritual principles of giving and receiving, I was bewildered when that very same week in which I was teaching about the Dead Sea to my small group, I heard Grant Jeffries on TBN state that the Dead Sea is actually the richest place on earth. Evidently, because of the actual dying process of the Dead Sea, rich deposits of minerals have been continually deposited layer upon layer on the bottom of the Dead Sea over thousands of years.

When I heard this and began to meditate upon it, I started to wonder why God would put the richest place on earth in a place called "dead." I couldn't understand why God would do this, so I asked Him about it in my prayer time; however, as each day passed, He wasn't answering my question. After about a week, I stopped seeking God for the answer. Then a strange thing happened to me later that week as I was shopping for Christmas presents in the local mall.

As I was walking down the mall, a young lady called out to me and asked if I had ever heard of the Dead Sea. A little startled and curious, I stopped to answer her question. At my affirmative response, she told me the story of how she was from Israel and that she was in the mall selling lotions specially made from the rich minerals of the Dead Sea. When she found out that I was married, she grabbed my hands to demonstrate the value of her product by rubbing the lotion on my hands and persuading me that it was the perfect gift for my wife. In fact, once she knew she had me sold, she inquired if my mother was alive and began to persuade me that a double purchase for my wife and my mom would be even more special.

I asked how much the mineral lotion was. Seeing I was concerned about price, the young sales lady told me that if I purchased two of the bottles, she would give me a third bottle free. So again, I asked her the price of the lotion. And as you might have guessed, those two little bottles of mineral lotions from the Dead Sea, the richest place on earth, were quite expensive. And the whole time I was being engaged with this little Jewish sales woman, I was internally asking the Lord what was this all about and why was this happening. I was wondering if I should buy the two bottles and get the third one free, but I didn't want to spend that much money. Plus I was thinking about the giving and receiving spiritual principle of the Dead Sea and wondering if God was trying to test me or teach me something about it.

Seeing that I was tormented in my decision, the little Jewish sales lady backed off and said, "How about you buy one and I give you the other one half price." That did it for me. I could buy one for my wife as a gift and then give her the other one so that she could give it to anyone else she wanted as a gift. This way the spiritual principle of giving and receiving that I have taught and illustrated by the reality of the Dead Sea would not be violated in my conscience, despite the fact that I was buying gifts that were made from the stagnant Dead Sea. Anyhow, when it was all said and done, I received an internal peace about the gifts I had bought straight from the Dead Sea.

Then later that day, as I was running on the treadmill at the gym, the Lord spoke to me in a small soft internal voice and said, "Do you still want to know why I put the richest place on earth in a place called dead?" Surprised at His question, I answered, "Yes, Lord, I really would like to know why You put the richest place on earth in a place called dead." Then He showed me a picture in my mind of Lazarus stepping out of a dead tomb when Jesus called him forth. With that as a backdrop, He then told me that the reason He put the richest place on earth in a place called dead is because what man calls dead, He calls alive! And that man is likened unto the Dead Sea, in that when man dies to himself, the riches that He, the Lord, buries inside us through the process, can come alive to bless others in very rich ways. This is why the richest place on earth is in a place called dead.

And with that answer, I was awestruck by what the Lord had just shared with me. After completing my run at the gym, I went immediately home to record the revelation in my personal faith journal so that I would not easily forget its meaning and impact to me. How awesome and great is the majesty of our living God that He would share such rich revelation with ordinary people like you and me!

In fact, this revelation from God that He personally shared with me about the Dead Sea became part of the inspiration for the title of this book, *Kings Come Forth!* It is my sincere desire that as you read the rest of this book, God will use it as an instrument to inspire you and other godly business leaders to accept His open invitation to come alive from dead spiritual places in your life and begin building the Lord's kingdom in the marketplace for His glory and His honor. Then, as you continually die to your flesh and become a genuine servant leader in the kingdom of God, I pray that the Lord will richly bless you and use you to do His kingdom bidding in the business community as His faithful kingdom ambassador for Christ.

2 The Spiritual Environment of the Current-day Kingdom Marketplace

And you shall remember the LORD your God, for it is He who gives you power to get wealth, that He may establish His covenant which He swore to your fathers, as it is this day. Then it shall be, if you by any means forget the LORD your God, and follow other gods, and serve them and worship them, I testify against you this day that you shall surely perish. As the nations which the LORD destroys before you, so you shall perish, because you would not be obedient to the voice of the LORD your God.

–Deuteronomy 8:18–20

TASKMASTER LEADERSHIP PRODUCES FEAR AND A CULTURE OF DISEMPOWERMENT

Unfortunately, in the business world today, people think that the person with the biggest title and the most authority is the most important person in an organization. However, in the kingdom of God, positional title and authority aren't the deciding factors for who are the most important people in an organization. As stated in the previous chapter, the people whom God thinks are the most important in an organization are the people who serve other people the best. However, because the spirit of the taskmaster seeks power, leaders that are driven by power create organizational structures that favor themselves and top-down positions of authority. With such organizational structures, the entire focus of the organization becomes centered on making the boss happy, and if he is not, the boss makes everyone else unhappy. The unspoken mantra of the taskmaster organization is "Happy boss, happy people," but the basic inherent problem with this mode of operation is that there is always something that can make the boss unhappy. Therefore, because the people within the organization know in their hearts that it is impossible to always make the boss happy, a spirit of fear begins to develop throughout the ranks. As a result, people actually become paralyzed into status quo thinking and ultimately feel disempowered with an inherent lack of trust in their leaders.

Taskmaster organizations produce an underlying spirit of fear within the hearts of the people because the people are constantly afraid of what may happen to them if they make the leaders at the top of the organization unhappy. Because taskmaster leaders actually think that the people on their team are there just to make them happy, they implement rigorous control tactics with punitive consequences for not meeting their expectations. "Management by Metrics," as I call it, is the taskmaster leader's primary tool to exercise authority over people and manipulate them into submission through fear, especially when the metrics to measure people's performance have not been established on a reasonable basis nor substantiated by good business principle. Let me further illustrate this spiritual reality in the workplace with the taskmaster leadership example of Pharaoh found in Exodus 5:1–14:

> Afterward Moses and Aaron went in and told Pharaoh, "Thus says the LORD God of Israel: 'Let My people go, that they may hold a feast to Me in the wilderness.'" And Pharaoh said, "Who is the LORD, that I should obey His voice to let Israel go? I do not know

the LORD, nor will I let Israel go." So they said, "The God of the Hebrews has met with us. Please, let us go three days' journey into the desert and sacrifice to the LORD our God, lest He fall upon us with pestilence or with the sword." Then the king of Egypt said to them, "Moses and Aaron, why do you take the people from their work? Get back to your labor." And Pharaoh said, "Look, the people of the land are many now, and you make them rest from their labor!" So the same day Pharaoh commanded the taskmasters of the people and their officers, saying, "You shall no longer give the people straw to make brick as before. Let them go and gather straw for themselves. And you shall lay on them the quota of bricks which they made before. You shall not reduce it. For they are idle; therefore they cry out, saying, 'Let us go and sacrifice to our God.' Let more work be laid on the men, that they may labor in it, and let them not regard false words." And the taskmasters of the people and their officers went out and spoke to the people, saying, "Thus says Pharaoh: 'I will not give you straw. Go, get yourselves straw where you can find it; yet none of your work will be reduced.'" So the people were scattered abroad throughout all the land of Egypt to gather stubble instead of straw. And the taskmasters forced them to hurry, saying, "Fulfill your work, your daily quota, as when there was straw." Also the officers of the children of Israel, whom Pharaoh's taskmasters had set over them, were beaten and were asked, "Why have you not fulfilled your task in making brick both yesterday and today, as before?"

BASIC TASKMASTER TACTIC: DOUBLE THE
QUOTA AND TAKE AWAY THE STRAW

When the business climate has no fear of God and places more importance on the production of numbers than the people producing the numbers, just as Pharaoh did by doubling the quota and taking away the straw, you know that the spirit of the taskmaster is leading the organization. Just think about our current-day marketplace. Where is the primary emphasis and focus of current-day kings, the business leaders of our corporations? Personally, I think their focus is far too keen on pleasing Wall Street investors in the pursuit of their own selfish benefit instead of pleasing God for the benefit of their customers and their employees. Organizations are rapidly replacing "Management by Principles" with "Management by Metrics" as a way of corporate life and operating culture in order to make their profit numbers and satisfy Wall Street. Unfortunately, pride, greed, and fear drive many executive leaders to stop at nothing to hit their target earnings and their six-figure bonuses.

I once heard an executive of a well-known worldwide company tell a group of company executives at a retreat that if the market wasn't going to appreciate their business with higher stock prices, then they were going to simply get out of that business. Whatever happened to the days of being in business because the business actually brought value to the people they served? An honest evaluation of our nation's corporate environment with a spiritual comparison to the example of Pharaoh in the days of Moses will hopefully shed light on the seriousness of this situation in corporate America. Until the business leaders of our corporations begin to understand and appreciate that the people in their companies don't just show up to maximize shareholder wealth, but rather show up to primarily fulfill God-given purpose on earth, our companies and our markets could experience some very serious, tumultuous times.

Now please do not misunderstand me and think that I am committing business heresy with such negative statements regarding organizations that strongly favor and embrace an overarching "Management by Metrics" operating culture. I am a certified public accountant by training and possess an undergraduate finance degree as well as a Master's of Business Administration degree. With my educational background and professional experiences, I most definitely understand the importance of establishing a strong culture of performance measurement within an organization's operating platform. However, in order for the platform to be built properly, I believe it must be built upon solid principles of good stewardship and management accountability and not management control tactics rooted in pride, greed, and fear.

When an organization builds an operating platform based on good stewardship and management accountability principles, I believe the leaders aggressively seek to measure performance and know the state of the company's business affairs. Furthermore, I believe that a good steward of a company's assets will be like the good shepherd of Proverbs 27:23—"Be[ing] diligent to know the state of your flocks, And attend[ing] to your herds"—through effective planning and regular performance measurement. Plus, I believe that the true test and measurement of a good company steward is a steady, consistent growth in the net worth of the company's assets under management.

However, contrary to what some business leaders might think, a company's greatest assets are not found in the numbers on the financial statements; they are rather found in the people employed by the company. Therefore, if the company leadership seeks to maximize the net worth and potential of its greatest assets by taking exceptional care of its people, then the financial net worth of the company will naturally and supernaturally take care of itself on the financial statements. Unfortunately, though, I think unchecked pride, greed, and fear are driving many business leaders in corporate America to be far more concerned with the bottom-line numbers than they are about the people on the bottom-line actually producing the numbers. With that said, I think the statement of Proverbs 29:2, "When the righteous are in authority, the people rejoice; But when a wicked man rules, the people groan," has never been more applicable regarding the current-day work environment for people in corporate America.

By the wisdom of Yogi Berra—"You can observe a lot by just watching"[1]—it is certainly disheartening to watch what is happening in the current-day business affairs of our nation. Congress packaged an $800 billion-dollar bailout plan for our banking and financial institutions to stabilize the backbone of our economy. The Dow Jones Industrial Average plummeted nearly 40 percent before it stabilized after nearly two years. The colossal business failures of Bear Stearns, Lehman Brothers, Fannie Mae, Freddie Mac, AIG, and Washington Mutual were vividly clear indicators that something was very wrong spiritually in our marketplace. On top of that, CNNMoney.com staff writer Aaron Smith reported that the CEO of Washington Mutual could in fact earn more than $18 million dollars in salary, bonus, and severance after less than three weeks on the job, according to the terms of his employment agreement with Washington Mutual, the largest failed bank in history.[2]

In our nation's current economic crisis, we don't just have a failure of leadership in business and a crisis of financial performance, we have a failure of *spiritual* leadership in business and a crisis of financial *stewardship*. Additional signs that the spiritual infrastructure of our corporations are crumbling from within are revealed in the following statistics on job satisfaction in America, as reported by the Conference Board Survey in August 2004:[3]

+ Only 49 percent of American workers are satisfied with their work

+ Only 14 percent are very satisfied with their work

+ 40 percent of workers feel disconnected from their employers

+ Two out of three workers do not feel motivated to drive their employer's business goals and objectives

+ 25 percent of employees are just "showing up to collect a paycheck"

As these facts and headlines confront us each day with the sobering reality of what is happening with the economic condition of the business communities in our nation, we must also soberly confront the reality of what is happening with the spiritual condition of the business leaders in our nation. For every occurrence happening in the natural world, there is a corresponding occurrence happening behind the scenes in the invisible supernatural world. With that said, could it be that our problems in the economy are related to an undermining of our spiritual foundations where business leaders in America have forgotten the biblical principles that our great country was founded upon as well as lost real respect and reverence for the Lord who prospered and blessed our nation beyond our Founding Fathers' wildest imaginations?

Do you remember what happened to the Israelites when the new Pharaoh who did not know Joseph came to power? Exodus 1:8 begins the historical record of the change in the spiritual climate surrounding the Israelites when the Bible records that "there arose a new king over Egypt, *who did not know Joseph*" (emphasis added). This is a significant statement in the Bible that can help explain what is happening in the spiritual environment of our current-day marketplace in America. Whether you know it or not, the Scriptures teach that the life of Joseph is an Old Testament foreshadowing of the life of Jesus.

Consider that Joseph was stripped of his robe and thrown into a pit. Similarly, Jesus was stripped of His robe and descended into the pit of hell after His death on the cross. Consider that Joseph was betrayed by Judah and sold to Midianite traders for twenty pieces of silver, who then later sold him as a slave at the going market price of thirty pieces of silver. Similarly, Jesus was betrayed by Judas (the same word as Judah in Hebrew) and sold for thirty pieces of silver. Consider that Joseph was brought to Egypt by Midianite traders carrying spices, balm, and myrrh. Similarly, the body of Jesus was brought to the tomb and embalmed with spices, myrrh, and aloes. Consider that God delivered Joseph from the pit. Similarly, God delivered Jesus from the pit of the grave after three days. These very direct similarities between the life and experiences of Joseph and that of Jesus are not coincidental by any means. In fact, they explicitly demonstrate how the natural aspects of life represented by Joseph in the Old Testament directly correspond and relate to the supernatural aspects of life represented by Jesus in the New Testament.

Understanding how the natural and the supernatural worlds can intersect, I am not surprised to find a very significant spiritual correlation when reading Exodus 1:8 in light of the natural and supernatural conditions of our current-day business climate in America. Reading the verse with a set of spiritual lenses provided by the Holy Spirit, I can clearly see how this verse has supernatural meaning and significance to our nation. Let me interject the spiritual insights of the verse related to the spiritual condition of business leadership in America as follows: "Now there arose a new king over Egypt [business leaders in America], who did not know Joseph [Jesus]." As you contemplate the meaning of this spiritually, can you see the similarities and relevance to our nation? Given the stark contrast between the Christian heritage of our nation and the reality of our current spiritual state, it should be no stretch to see that the current-day kings of our land—business leaders—have risen to power, and yet unfortunately, many, like Pharaoh, *do not know Jesus* as Lord.

With the systematic attack by secular humanists to remove prayer from our classrooms and the Ten Commandments from our courtrooms, it is no wonder that the spiritual climate of our nation is falling down at every level, including the business community. However, regardless of what the spiritually blind among us would have us believe, it is clear that our Founding Fathers put their faith and trust in almighty God. By their personal signing and adoption of the Declaration of Independence on July 4, 1776, our Founding Fathers publicly declared their faith and trust in almighty God as evidenced by the words penned by Thomas Jefferson in the most powerful document ever written:

> We hold these truths to be self-evident, that all men are created equal, that they are endowed by their Creator with certain unalienable rights....We, therefore, the Representatives of the United States of America, in General Congress, Assembled, appealing to the

Supreme Judge of the world for the rectitude of our
intentions....And for the support of this declaration,
with a firm reliance on the protection of Divine Provi-
dence, we mutually pledge to each other our lives, our
fortunes and our sacred honor.[4]

And just in case you might be wondering whether Thomas
Jefferson believed in Jesus Christ as Lord, you can find that he
most certainly did in his National Prayer for Peace before a
throng of elected officials on March 4, 1805:

Almighty God, Who has given us this good land for
our heritage; We humbly beseech Thee that we may
always prove ourselves a people mindful of Thy favor
and glad to do Thy will. Bless our land with hono-
rable ministry, sound learning, and pure manners.
Save us from violence, discord, and confusion, from
pride and arrogance and from every evil way. Defend
our liberties, and fashion into one united people, the
multitude brought hither out of many kindreds and
tongues. Endow with Thy spirit wisdom those whom
in Thy name we entrust the authority of government,
that there may be justice and peace at home, and that
through obedience to Thy law, we may show forth Thy
praise among the nations of the earth. In time of pros-
perity fill our hearts with thankfulness, and in the day
of trouble, suffer not our trust in Thee to fail; all of
which we ask through Jesus Christ our Lord. Amen.[5]

Just imagine what could happen in our nation if our business
leaders possessed the same kind of spiritual backbone and forti-
tude as our Founding Fathers. If they did, our business leaders
would be unafraid to pledge their lives, fortunes, and sacred honor
to uphold the principles of the Declaration of Independence

through public prayer in the name of Jesus Christ our Lord. As promised in 2 Chronicles 7:14, I truly believe that God will heal our land as well as our national economy as we, business leaders called by God's name, humble ourselves and pray, seek His face, and turn from our wicked ways. To see this happen, each godly business leader in America must search his heart and repent from doing business the world's way and begin stewarding business God's way as a servant leader in His kingdom.

SERVANT LEADERSHIP PRODUCES FAITH AND A CULTURE OF EMPOWERMENT

Somewhere in the course of my study and readings, I came across an illustrated tombstone in a Dilbert cartoon stating that the deceased would have done some really neat things, but his boss wouldn't let him! I wonder how many people in America's companies today feel just like the Dilbert character. I don't know the numbers or the percentages, but based on the statistics gathered from the Conference Board Survey shared earlier, my intuition tells me that it is far too many. In fact, in 1998, the Franklin Covey Company did a survey of employees in corporate America and asked them what they thought were the different cultural factors that were holding back quality in our corporate institutions. Not surprisingly, more than 50 percent of the respondents thought that the top three factors holding back quality were (1) employees don't trust senior management, (2) poor communication with management, and (3) people are not empowered by management.[6] Now there is something I want to make clear about my thoughts regarding authority and leadership. While I have been direct and frank about what I believe to be the current state of affairs in business leadership, please understand that in no way do I advocate showing disrespect for the business leaders whom God has given the authority to lead and direct us in the business affairs of our organizations. In fact, quite the contrary; the Bible is clear in Daniel 2:21 that the Lord Himself removes kings and raises up kings; therefore, we must respect whom God has placed in authority over us. And not only that, the apostle Paul commands us to pray for those in authority in 1 Timothy 2:1–2, "Therefore I exhort first of all that supplications, prayers, intercessions, and giving of thanks be made for all men, for kings and all who are in authority, that we may lead a quiet and peaceable life in all godliness and reverence." As you can see, respect for our business leaders, regardless of their spiritual condition, is required of us by God.

Authority vs. Empowerment

One morning during my devotion time, I was praying about a particular situation at work where I felt that one of the employees on my team was taking advantage of me and not really giving me an appropriate level of respect as their leader. I was complaining to God about the fact that I had given so much to empower this particular person, but somehow wasn't being appreciated or respected for the role I was playing in their development and empowerment.

So as I took the situation to the Lord in prayer, He asked me a very odd and direct question. In a still small voice He asked me what was more important, empowerment or authority. As I pondered His question, I replied to Him that I thought empowerment was very important. In fact, I reminded Him of how much I had given in leadership time and focus to empower others to be all that He had created them to be. But then, at the same time, I told the Lord that I knew authority was important as well, but was cautious about authority since I observed many authority figures inappropriately exercising their authority over others.

The Lord then spoke very plainly to me, stating, "There can be no empowerment without there first being authority that empowers." And then He got real personal with me: "But I don't know why you are so concerned about this situation of disrespect from one of your employees, because the way that person is treating you is exactly the same way you have been treating Me. I have empowered you with gifts and talents to make a difference in life, but you have completely ignored My authority in your life and have disrespected Me in many ways. Why don't you get this straight first, and then worry about that problem with your employee?" Immediately the Lord's direct whisper cut to my heart and I knew it was true. In brokenness before Him, I repented for all of my foolish ways toward Him and asked Him to forgive me for my sin of irreverent disrespect of His authority in my life.

As I transparently share this very personal matter in my relationship with the Lord, perhaps you are thinking that you have treated the Lord in the same disrespectful way that I had been doing. If that is the case, then all you need to do is the same thing that I did. Get on your knees, confess your sin to Him, and ask Him to forgive you and cleanse you. The Bible says in Acts 10:34 that God is no respecter of persons; therefore, if He forgave my sin, He will certainly forgive you as well. Furthermore, 1 John 1:9 states, "If we confess our sins, He is faithful and just to forgive us our sins and to cleanse us from all unrighteousness." And lastly, God also promises that not only will He forgive us and cleanse us, but in James 4:8 He promises that He will also draw near to us as we draw near to Him. What an awesome promise from God!

THE LEGACY QUESTION

As a business leader responsible to lead your team and help fulfill its destiny, will your leadership efforts create a team legacy of fear and "can't do" disempowerment or will your leadership efforts create a team legacy of faith and "can do" empowerment? Personally, I have a holy, righteous hatred for the spirit of fear and the spirit of can't because they rob people of their destiny and destroy their legacy. As a matter of Jewish legacy, the children of Israel experienced a major problem with the spirits of fear and can't after they were released from the Egyptian bondage of Pharaoh.

Before stepping into the Promised Land and their destiny as a nation, Moses did as any wise leader would do before taking a big step into unchartered territory. He sent forth leaders to evaluate the land, gather important information, and assess their options. The Bible records in Numbers 13:26–33 the report of the twelve leaders representing each of the twelve tribes of Israel who were sent by Moses to spy out the Promised Land:

> Now they departed and came back to Moses and Aaron and all the congregation of the children of Israel in the Wilderness of Paran, at Kadesh; they brought back word to them and to all the congregation, and showed them the fruit of the land. Then they told him, and said: "We went to the land where you sent us. It truly flows with milk and honey, and this is its fruit. Nevertheless the people who dwell in the land are strong; the cities are fortified and very large; moreover we saw the descendants of Anak there. The Amalekites dwell in the land of the South; the Hittites, the Jebusites, and the Amorites dwell in the mountains; and the Canaanites dwell by the sea and along the banks

of the Jordan." Then Caleb quieted the people before Moses, and said, "Let us go up at once and take possession [spirit of can do], for we are well able to overcome it [spirit of faith]." But the men who had gone up with him said, "We are not able to go up against the people [spirit of can't], for they are stronger than we [spirit of fear]." And they gave the children of Israel a bad report of the land which they had spied out, saying, "The land through which we have gone as spies is a land that devours its inhabitants, and all the people whom we saw in it are men of great stature. There we saw the giants (the descendants of Anak came from the giants); and we were like grasshoppers in our own sight, and so we were in their sight."

When leaders allow a spirit of fear to dominate and permeate the thought consciousness of their teams, the spirit of can't is sure to grow, stealing purpose and destiny from many. Through the spirit of can't, an entire generation of Israelites wandered and died in the desert rather than possessing the Promised Land of God. This is why I have a holy, righteous hatred for the spirit of can't.

On a side note, do you know that it's not the power of hate that is the biggest enemy to the advancement of God's kingdom on earth? The truth is that without the ability to hate there can be no ability to truly love, and it is only true love that can advance the kingdom of God. Now that's a powerful thought to meditate upon. With that said and understood, we must also understand that the biggest enemy to the advancement of the kingdom of God on earth is actually the power of complacency which neither hates nor loves.

God hates complacency! Revelation 3:14–17 emphatically declares His personal disdain for it. "And to the angel of the church of the Laodiceans write, 'These things says the Amen, the Faithful and True Witness, the Beginning of the creation of God: I know your works, that you are neither cold nor hot. I could wish you were cold or hot. So then, because you are lukewarm, and neither cold nor hot, I will vomit you out of My mouth.'" Although this may read harshly, we must know that God loves us so much that He tells us the truth always—which is the only way we can be truly free to love what He loves and hate what He hates, doing His will on earth as His kingdom ambassadors.

As believers in Christ, His kingdom ambassadors on earth, we must hate the power of complacency and overcome the enemy spirit of can't in our lives. Otherwise the destiny of our generation hangs in the balance today and forever. By truly loving the Lord's Holy Spirit of "can do" empowerment, we can build His kingdom on earth as it is in heaven, positively impacting the course of our nation for this generation and the generations to come. However, to do so, we will have to bury the spirit of can't in our lives and fully embrace the Lord's "can do" Holy Spirit.

HERE LIES I CAN'T

One day, when I had just assumed responsibility of the health and fitness division of the organization employing me, I learned of a true story about our aquatics director, which powerfully illustrates the power of possessing a positive, "can-do" spirit. To help his swim team become one of the best swim teams in our nation, he inspired their team to actually bury the spirit of can't. He did so by having each team member personally sign a large rock with a black permanent marker. He then went to the garden at the head of the pool and dug a deep hole, placing the rock with all of their names on it in the hole. He then buried the rock and placed a tombstone garden sign in the mud that read,

"Here Lies I Can't," to be a constant reminder to the team that the spirit of can't was dead and buried, having no part or place in their team life.

I actually don't know how the director came up with this idea; however, it is no doubt an extraordinary life application of binding up the spirit of can't and creating a team culture of "cando" empowerment. In essence, the director of our swim team was unleashing within his team a freedom to dream big, swim large, and reach for the gold standard of swimming excellence.

If he could do this with his team by having faith in their natural gifting and talents, just imagine how much more we can do in life if we have faith in God to add His "super" to our natural gifting and abilities.

Philippians 4:13 states, "I can do all things through Christ who strengthens me"; therefore, as believers in Christ leading in the marketplace, we are supernaturally empowered by the Spirit of Christ living inside of us to create business cultures of empowerment that unleash business men and women to dream big, live large, and reach for the gold standard of business excellence, completely fulfilling their life purpose and becoming all that God created them to be on earth. I personally believe that there is no greater tragedy to the heart of God than for Him to see people created in His image living life less than what He died on the cross to give them. In John 10:10, the Lord Himself states, "I have come that they may have life, and that they may have it more abundantly." And, believe it or not, that heart desire of God is true for every person on earth, even people doing kingdom life in the business marketplace.

3

The Three Kingdom Offices of Godly Spiritual Authority

But we have this treasure in earthen vessels,
that the excellence of the power may be of
God and not of us. We are hard-pressed on
every side, yet not crushed; we are perplexed,
but not in despair; persecuted, but not
forsaken; struck down, but not destroyed.

–2 Corinthians 4:7–9

WHEN READING THE Old Testament of the Bible, it is clearly evident that God chose to communicate His will and govern the affairs of His people through three primary offices of authority: the priest, the prophet, and the king. As such, it's important we understand that each person in the Old Testament having the responsibility of one of these roles was especially chosen by God and anointed by Him to carry out His purposes through the duties and responsibilities of that particular office. *Easton's Bible Dictionary* defines each office in the context of the early Hebrew nation as follows:[1]

+ *Priest*: one who represents the Jewish people before God and offers sacrifices as prescribed in the law of God

+ *Prophet*: one who speaks for God in His name and by His authority

+ *King*: one invested with authority to rule the Jewish nation as a servant representative of Jehovah God, the one true King of Israel.

THE OFFICE OF PRIEST

The Old Testament outlines in Exodus 29:42–44 the daily duties of Aaron and his sons consecrated by God to serve Him as priests alone. God spoke these words:

> These burnt offerings are to be made each day from generation to generation. Offer them in the LORD's presence at the Tabernacle entrance; there I will meet with you and speak with you. I will meet the people of Israel there, in the place made holy by my glorious presence. Yes, I will consecrate the Tabernacle and the altar, and *I will consecrate Aaron and his sons to serve me as priests.*
>
> —NLT, EMPHASIS ADDED

It is clear that God ordained and consecrated Aaron and his sons to be the priests of the tabernacle.

Furthermore, of the twelve tribes of Israel, God separated only one tribe unto Himself to serve Him in the priesthood. It was actually the smallest tribe of all—the tribe of Levi. Numbers 3:5–10 records the Lord's command to Moses regarding the separation of the tribe of Levi to serve in the priesthood:

> And the LORD spoke to Moses, saying: "Bring the tribe
> of Levi near, and present them before Aaron the priest,
> that they may serve him. And they shall attend to his
> needs and the needs of the whole congregation before
> the tabernacle of meeting, to do the work of the taber-
> nacle. Also they shall attend to all the furnishings of
> the tabernacle of meeting, and to the needs of the chil-
> dren of Israel, to do the work of the tabernacle. And
> you shall give the Levites to Aaron and his sons; they
> are given entirely to him from among the children of
> Israel. So you shall appoint Aaron and his sons, and
> they shall attend to their priesthood; but the outsider
> who comes near shall be put to death."

Therefore, we can see from Scripture that the Lord took
the role of the priesthood very seriously by selecting a special
people, the Levites, to be set apart and consecrated unto Him
to serve in the office and authority of the priesthood. The Lord
considered this matter so seriously He commanded that anyone
attempting to serve in the priesthood outside of the special
elect tribe of Levi was to be put to death. In short, the role and
authority given to the priesthood by God is reserved and not to
be taken lightly.

THE OFFICE OF PROPHET

The Old Testament outlines in Deuteronomy 18:18–22 the role
and responsibility of a prophet.

> I [the Lord] will raise up for them [the people of God]
> a Prophet [Jesus, the perfect prophet] like you [Moses]
> from among their brethren, and will put My words
> in His mouth, and He shall speak to them all that I
> command Him. And it shall be that whoever will not

hear My words, which He speaks in My name, I will
require it of him. But the prophet who presumes to
speak a word in My name, which I have not commanded
him to speak, or who speaks in the name of other gods,
that prophet shall die. And if you say in your heart,
"How shall we know the word which the LORD has not
spoken?"—when a prophet speaks in the name of the
LORD, if the thing does not happen or come to pass,
that is the thing which the LORD has not spoken; the
prophet has spoken it presumptuously; you shall not be
afraid of him."

As you can see, based on these scripture verses, God takes
the role of prophet just as serious as he takes the role of priest.
As God's personal spokesman, the prophet of God only has the
authority to speak exactly what God tells him or her to speak to
the people—nothing more and nothing less. In fact, God takes
His Word so seriously that God told the people that if the thing
which a prophet speaks does not come to pass, that prophet is to
be considered a false prophet and he or she shall die. To represent God and speak on His behalf is no lighthearted matter; it
carries a tremendous weight and moral responsibility.

In 2 Peter 1:20–21 (NLT), the apostle Peter affirms that the
source of all prophecy in Scripture is God Himself, stating,
"Above all, you must realize that no prophecy in Scripture ever
came from the prophet's own understanding, or from human
initiative. No, those prophets were moved by the Holy Spirit,
and they spoke from God." In contrast, the false prophet
speaking on behalf of himself knew that he was going to die if
what he spoke did not come to pass—no ordinary performance
review for certain.

Furthermore, in chapter 2:1–3 (NLT), the apostle Peter warns
the people of God regarding the danger of false prophets, stating:

But there were also false prophets in Israel, just as there will be false teachers among you. They will cleverly teach destructive heresies and even deny the Master who bought them. In this way, they will bring sudden destruction on themselves. Many will follow their evil teaching and shameful immorality. And because of these teachers, the way of truth will be slandered. In their greed they will make up clever lies to get hold of your money. But God condemned them long ago, and their destruction will not be delayed.

Unfortunately, just like the Old Testament times, there are false prophets among us who teach deception and slander the truth for greed and love of money. And if that were not bad enough, the real tragedy is that people who are as sheep without a shepherd are led away into the deceitfulness of sin and rebellion. The father of lies, satan himself, is working in the lives of these blind false guides to lead people away from the truth that can set them free. I pray in Jesus' name that Jehovah Roi, the Lord—our Shepherd—will break every yoke of deception and false teaching within the pastures of His people by the light of His Word and truth spoken through His special elect anointed ambassadors of the gospel.

THE OFFICE OF KING

Before Israel ever had a king to rule over them, the Lord Jehovah was their King. He communicated with them, ruled them, and judged them through His prophets. However, when Samuel the prophet grew old, the scriptures record in 1 Samuel 8:1–9 that the children of Israel complained to him about the dishonesty of his sons and requested that he appoint a king to rule over them like all of the other nations.

Now it came to pass when Samuel was old that he made his sons judges over Israel. The name of his first-born was Joel, and the name of his second, Abijah; they were judges in Beersheba. But his sons did not walk in his ways; they turned aside after dishonest gain, took bribes, and perverted justice. Then all the elders of Israel gathered together and came to Samuel at Ramah, and said to him, "Look, you are old, and your sons do not walk in your ways. Now make us a king to judge us like all the nations." But the thing displeased Samuel when they said, "Give us a king to judge us." So Samuel prayed to the LORD. And the LORD said to Samuel, "Heed the voice of the people in all that they say to you; for they have not rejected you, but they have rejected Me, that I should not reign over them. According to all the works which they have done since the day that I brought them up out of Egypt, even to this day—with which they have forsaken Me and served other gods—so they are doing to you also. Now therefore, heed their voice. However, you shall solemnly forewarn them, and show them the behavior of the king who will reign over them."

With counsel from God, the prophet Samuel obeyed, appointing the very first king, whose name was Saul, to rule over the kingdom of Israel. With the introduction of this new office in God's organizational chart of authority, He ordained a three tier government of the people with three separate and distinct branches of kingdom authority: the legislative branch (priests), the judicial branch (prophets, also called judges), and the executive branch (kings). It should be no wonder that the government of the people of the United States of America is the most effective governmental structure in the world; it offers three tiers of checks and balances modeled exactly after God's kingdom authority structure that God ordained to rule His kingdom on earth. Praise God for the wisdom, knowledge, and understanding of our God-fearing Founding Fathers of America.

THREE ROLES IN ONE: THE WAY, THE TRUTH, AND THE LIFE

So as you can see, all throughout the Old Testament people were anointed and designated by God in the offices of priest, prophet, and king to lead and guide His people according to His ways and His will. When the people honored God, respecting His elect authority on earth and following after His will, He blessed them and protected them with His favor. However, as you quickly discover reading the Old Testament, the people did not always choose to honor God, respect His elect authority on earth, and follow after His will. All too often they rather chose to follow after their own independent will and sinful ways, which resulted in tragic consequences of bondage and captivity—every time. This is not at all any different than the same tragic consequences today of following after our own independent will and sinful ways rather than choosing to love God with our whole heart and live according to His ways.

And while the tragic consequences of our sin are still the same today as they were in the Old Testament, there is most definitely one major difference between our day and that of the Old Testament. We, the people of God, are not governed and led by the Old Testament law of God, but rather the far better New Testament grace of God, through the death and resurrection life of Jesus Christ, our Lord and Savior. In the Old Testament, the authority structures of priest, prophet, and king were established by God to administer His will through the Law of God given to us by Moses written on tablets of stone by the Ten Commandments on Mount Sinai. Today the authority structures of priest, prophet, and king remain the same; however, in the New Testament they are established to administer God's will through the grace of God freely given to us by Jesus and written on the tablets of our heart by His shed blood on the cross.

In John 14:6, Jesus makes an amazing declaration to Thomas, one of the twelve apostles. He frankly states, "I am the way, the truth, and the life. No one comes to the Father except through Me." This means that in the New Testament era of grace, God left nothing undone and He covered every base in the kingdom through the life of His beloved Son, Jesus, in whom He was well pleased. As the *way*, the *truth*, and the *life*, Jesus is our perfect Priest showing us the one true *way* to the kingdom of God, perfect Prophet speaking the whole *truth* of the kingdom of God with unconditional love toward us, and perfect King developing the *life* of God in each of us as believers in the kingdom of God.

Furthermore, when asked by the Pharisees about the coming kingdom of God as recorded in Luke 17:20–21, Jesus tells them, "The kingdom of God does not come with observation; nor will they say, 'See here!' or 'See there!' *For indeed, the kingdom of God is within you*" (emphasis added.) Wow! This means that when we surrender our lives to Jesus, He not only comes to live inside us, but He also brings the whole kingdom package with Him because He *is* the whole kingdom package. Think about it! Jesus Christ—our perfect priest, our perfect prophet, and our perfect king—all three branches of God's perfect kingdom takes up residence in each one of us.

Is this too unthinkable? Well, let the apostle Paul settle it with his Holy Spirit-inspired letter to the Galatian believers. In verses 20 and 21 of Galatians chapter 2, Paul writes, "I have been crucified with Christ; *it is no longer I who live, but Christ lives in me*; and the life which I now live in the flesh I live by faith in the Son of God, who loved me and gave Himself for me" (emphasis added). Now, there you have it: Jesus Christ Himself lives inside of us by faith in Him, and that means the whole perfect kingdom package lives inside of us. As that truth becomes manifested in each of our lives by the indwelling work of the Holy Spirit in us, there is no reason why we should not see the Lord's prayer fulfilled in our lives: "Thy kingdom come, thy will be done, on earth as it is in heaven!"

4 The King's Anointing and Purpose

He asked life from You, and You gave it to
him—Length of days forever and ever. His glory
is great in Your salvation; Honor and majesty
You have placed upon him. For You have made
him most blessed forever; You have made him
exceedingly glad with Your presence. For the
king trusts in the LORD, And through the mercy
of the Most High he shall not be moved.
                                        —Psalm 21:1–7

WHERE IS THE KINGDOM OF GOD
IN THE MARKETPLACE?

So if the kingdom of God lives inside each one of us as believers
in Christ, why don't we see more of God's kingdom in our
everyday, real-world lives? More specifically, what has happened
to God's kingdom in the marketplace? From Wall Street to
Main Street, where is God's kingdom?

Well, from the previous chapter we already know that God's
kingdom is in the hearts and minds of every believer in Him;
therefore, the fact that we don't see much of God's kingdom in
our everyday lives is not a matter of whether or not God is actually there, because He is. In fact, one of His names, Jehovah
Shammah—the Lord is there—declares that He is already
there, including on Wall Street and Main Street; however,
I believe that the reason we don't see more of His kingdom

manifesting in our natural business world is because the kings on Wall Street and Main Street—our modern-day business leaders of the marketplace—have lost their vision and revelation of God's kingdom and His purpose for their lives.

Proverbs 29:18 states, "Where there is no revelation, the people cast off restraint; But happy is he who keeps the law." Consequently, there doesn't seem to be much godly restraint in the marketplace because today's business leaders have no vision of what it means to bring the freedom reign of the Cross to the business community. Instead, every leader on Wall Street and Main Street is doing what he or she thinks is right in their own mind, as it was in the days described in Judges 21:25: "In those days there was no king in Israel; everyone did what was right in his own eyes." Sadly, without any vision to bring the values of the kingdom to the marketplace in real-life, practical ways, we will continue to see very little of God's kingdom values and influence in the marketplace. On the other hand, if we can effectively reach the business leader in the marketplace—the place where modern-day kings live everyday of the week, we can then effectively build the kingdom in the marketplace with the values of the kingdom.

I will go even as far as to say that until business leaders in the marketplace receive real revelation from the Word of God regarding their full-time, God-ordained purpose and role in the kingdom, the church body of Christ will fail to see God's kingdom fully manifest itself on earth as it is in heaven. I realize that such a statement is bold; however, I make the statement in the boldness of Christ, not me. And to be even more frank in the Holy Spirit, I believe modern-day kings in the marketplace have more purpose in the kingdom of God than to be fundraisers for the church and part-time participants in the ministry. Again, I realize that this is a bold statement; however, unless someone has the courage in God to bring this matter to the attention of godly church leaders secure in their own roles and purpose in Christ, far too many churches will continue to unknowingly make kings in their midst feel as though the full-time roles they play in the marketplace don't have much kingdom value, except to be a source of giving to the vision of the church and provide an opportunity to participate in the ministry on a part-time basis. Such a view that only ascribes value to kings in this manner seriously marginalizes the king and disrespects his full-time, God-ordained created purpose in the marketplace as well as terribly limits God's kingdom influence in the business world. Together, in a spirit of respectful partnership, priests and kings must change this, if we truly desire to transform the business community with the values of the kingdom of God.

Randy Alcorn writes in his book *The Treasure Principle*, "Christians should love their pastors and support them financially (Galatians 6:6), but first and foremost we give to God (2 Corinthians 8:5). Before anything else, giving is an act of worship."[1] To fully understand my spirit in this matter, please know that I honestly and sincerely thank God for the wonderful anointed pastors in my spiritual family who are not only secure in their role and purpose in Christ, but also possess an awesome godly vision to reach people and build lives in the kingdom of God. My family and I are huge beneficiaries of the calling of God on their lives; and as a result, we are indebted with tremendous gratitude towards God for what He has done in our family through His faithfulness and the faithfulness of our pastors to reach people and build lives in our community.

Furthermore, in my former industry role as a king in the marketplace, it has been my sincere pleasure to do kingdom life with my pastors, committing my time, talents, and treasure to support them financially and do my part to make their God-given vision happen in Christ. Plus, now that I am a full-time member of the leadership team at my church, serving as chief administrative officer and pastor of business leaders in the marketplace, I am excited about the opportunities to work directly with business leaders and effectively equip them to build God's kingdom in the business community. And because God is way bigger than any of us can ever think or imagine, I believe that God's vision and plan for His kingdom includes a full-time, God-ordained role for everyone, including kings, to reach people, build lives, and make a significant difference in His kingdom. But at the end of the day, regardless of the specific purpose and role that we all play in the kingdom of God, I agree with Randy Alcorn that for all of us, our giving is first and foremost an act of obedience and worship to God, not a role we play in the kingdom. It should simply be our good pleasure to give to God because God loved us so much that He first gave everything to us in His only begotten Son, the Lord Jesus Christ.

And just to make it clear regarding my personal heart attitude towards giving, I wholeheartedly believe in giving from a grateful heart and do so in word and deed. In fact, my financial records and my faith-filled attitude of giving personally demonstrates that my wife and I are cheerful givers to the house of God. We faithfully give a tithe of our income from an obedient heart toward God, and we also give offerings above our tithe as the Holy Spirit leads us to do so. Simply put, giving tithes and offerings is a test of the heart for every believer regardless of the role and purpose we each play in the kingdom.

For instance, an anointed, godly plumber uses his God-given talents to plumb with excellence because he was created by God to plumb; but he gives the first of all his increase in tithes and offerings because he simply loves God with an obedient, faith-filled heart towards Him. Similarly, an anointed, godly preacher uses his God-given talents to preach with excellence because he was created by God to preach; but he gives the first of all his increase in tithes and offerings because he simply loves God with an obedient faith-filled heart towards Him. The same is true for anyone in the kingdom of God—we give because we love God and are obedient to His Word. Jesus affirms this in Matthew 6:21, stating, "For where your treasure is, there your heart will be also." Therefore, as kings and priests in God's kingdom, we cheerfully give to the kingdom for no other purpose than to love God with an obedient faith-filled heart towards Him.

Besides, the Lord is so awesome and gracious that while He tests our heart towards Him with 10 percent of the income He provides—just big enough to matter and not so big that it can't be done—He allows us to also test His heart toward us in this matter. Malachi 3:10–12 highlights God's challenge to test Him and receive the reward of the tithe test, stating:

> "Bring all the tithes into the storehouse, That there may be food in My house, And *try Me* now in this," Says the LORD of hosts, "If I will not open for you the windows of heaven And pour out for you such blessing That there will not be room enough to receive it. And I will rebuke the devourer for your sakes, So that he will not destroy the fruit of your ground, Nor shall the vine fail to bear fruit for you in the field," Says the LORD of hosts; "And all nations will call you blessed, For you will be a delightful land," says the LORD of hosts.
>
> —EMPHASIS ADDED

Please understand that the tithe is not the church's way to get money from people, nor does God need our money either—everything already belongs to Him. The tithe is simply God's way to test our hearts in obedience to Him as well as God's way to bless the fruit of our work beyond our own natural abilities and gifts. We simply can't out give God; He won't let you and I do it. In fact, He dares us to take Him at His Word and try Him with our tithes and our offerings.

When it comes to God's kingdom principles of giving and receiving, it is most comforting to know that one day of God's supernatural favor and blessing is worth more than a lifetime of toil and labor in our own natural strength. As kings in the marketplace, just imagine what could be done in Christ's strength if kings truly believed God and actually took Him for His Word. While this may sound like a foreign concept to many in the marketplace, believing God and taking Him for His Word is exactly how our nation was founded and how it became the most blessed nation in the world.

The Prayer of Our Nation's First President, George Washington

Before there ever were the markets on Wall Street and the modern-day kings of corporate America, the free citizens of our newly formed country democratically elected its very first "king," President George Washington. After his inauguration, it is reported that he walked down Wall Street to St. Paul's Chapel, still standing today across the street from the former Twin Towers of the World Trade Center, to pray to the Lord. One of his prayers prayed on June 8, 1783, is captured on a plaque hanging in the chapel today:

Almighty God: We make our earnest prayer that Thou wilt keep the United States in Thy holy protection; that Thou wilt incline the hearts of the citizens to cultivate a spirit of subordination and obedience to government; and entertain a brotherly affection and love for one another and for their fellow citizens of the United States at large. And finally that Thou wilt most graciously be pleased to dispose us all to do justice, to love mercy, and to demean ourselves with that charity, humility and pacific temper of mind, which were the characteristics of the Divine Author of our blessed religion, and without an humble imitation of whose example in these things we can never hope to be a happy nation. Grant our supplication we beseech Thee through Jesus Christ, our Lord. Amen.[2]

President George Washington, a mighty man of God and our nation's first elected king, knew that the happiness of our nation depended upon God's grace to make us a people who loved one another with brotherly affection and who would become imitators of His justice, mercy, charity, and humility. As our elected king, President George Washington modeled this example as evidenced by his supplication to God through Jesus Christ, our Lord. With his presidential leadership and kingly anointing, our nation became the most favored nation among nations, taking more ground for the kingdom of God than any other nation in the history of the world. President George Washington knew that his role and responsibility as our nation's first ever king was first to love God with his whole heart, mind, and soul; second, to love his neighbor as himself; and third, to possess the land and build the kingdom of God in accordance with His virtues, principles, and will, as written in His Holy Word.

THE KING'S PURPOSE: POSSESS THE LAND AND BUILD THE KINGDOM

The way that our nation possessed the land of America and built the kingdom of God within its borders and territories is not much different than the way that Joshua and the children of Israel possessed their Promised Land. Led by Joshua, they had to fight for the land with the mighty hand of the Lord as their shield and victory in battle. In fact, Joshua 18:3–7 records Joshua's admonition to the leaders of each tribe who had not yet gone to take possession of the land to go and possess it.

> Then Joshua said to the children of Israel: "How long will you neglect to go and possess the land which the LORD God of your fathers has given you? Pick out from among you three men for each tribe, and I will send them; they shall rise and go through the land, survey it according to their inheritance, and come back to me. And they shall divide it into seven parts. Judah shall remain in their territory on the south, and the house of Joseph shall remain in their territory on the north. You shall therefore survey the land in seven parts and bring the survey here to me, that I may cast lots for you here before the LORD our God. But the Levites have no part among you, for the priesthood of the LORD is their inheritance. And Gad, Reuben, and half the tribe of Manasseh have received their inheritance beyond the Jordan on the east, which Moses the servant of the LORD gave them."

Notice that Joshua told the leaders of the tribes—in essence, the king of each tribe—to go and take the land that God had given them. This command was his directive to the kings and not the priests. In truth, he clarified the matter even further by stating that the priest would have no part among them in taking the land as an inheritance because their inheritance was to be set apart as the priesthood of the Lord. In other words, their hands were not for taking ground or making war. Taking ground and possessing the land in battle was the leadership responsibility and role of the kings. This has tremendous spiritual implications for the role and responsibility that our modern-day kings are to play in building God's kingdom today.

Scripture further supports the notion that the kings were assigned the responsibility for waging war and taking ground in the kingdom. Let's go back and look at the twelve spies that Moses sent out to spy the land forty years prior to Joshua leading the kings of each tribe into battle to actually take possession of the Promised Land. Remember that God directed Moses to identify and send out twelve spies—heads of the children of Israel—representing each of the twelve tribes. Numbers 13:1–2 records His command to Moses, "And the Lord spoke to Moses, saying, 'Send men to spy out the land of Canaan, which I am giving to the children of Israel; from each tribe of their fathers you shall send a man, every one a leader among them.'"

So let's name each spy and the tribe they represented as recorded in Numbers 13:3–15:

1. Tribe of Reuben—Shammua

2. Tribe of Simeon—Shaphat

3. Tribe of Judah—Caleb

4. Tribe of Issachar—Igal

5. Tribe of Ephraim, the son of Joseph—Hoshea (Joshua)

6. Tribe of Benjamin—Palti

7. Tribe of Zebulun—Gaddiel

8. Tribe of Manasseh, the son of Joseph—Gaddi

9. Tribe of Dan—Ammiel

10. Tribe of Asher—Sethur

11. Tribe of Naphtali—Nahbi

12. Tribe of Gad—Geuel

To identify the twelve sons of Israel who fathered each of their respective tribes, 1 Chronicles 2:1–2 records, "These were the sons of Israel: Reuben, Simeon, Levi, Judah, Issachar, Zebulun, Dan, Joseph, Benjamin, Naphtali, Gad, and Asher." When comparing this list of the twelve sons of Israel recorded here to the list of twelve tribes represented by the spies listed above and recorded in Numbers, do you notice anything odd?

The tribe of Joseph is actually represented twice through his two sons, Ephraim and Manasseh, while the tribe of Levi is not represented at all. For me, this is a huge revelation supporting the truth that God has placed the responsibility and authority for taking the land on the kings of the kingdom and not the priests. Unfortunately, our current-day traditional authority structures in the church do very little to recognize the spiritual authority and kingdom responsibility of the kings in the church to take the land for the kingdom of God.

As a result, I personally believe that the king's full-time role and responsibility for taking the land has been diminished to part-time participation in the ministry rather than full-time anointed leadership in the army of the Lord. As such, this does not fully engage the kings in their rightful responsibilities, nor is it God's full intent for the role of the king in His kingdom business. I'll emphasize this once more because I am fully persuaded in the Holy Spirit that kings have more purpose in the kingdom of God than to raise money for the church through business and serve in the ministry on a part-time basis. As a matter of spirit-led conviction, I know deep within me that the greater purpose of kings in the kingdom of God is to fully serve the Lord in their full-time roles as kings, completely taking the land—every sphere of marketplace influence—for the kingdom of God, in the power, might, and strength of the Lord.

THE KING'S DOMAIN AUTHORITY

Romans 13:1–3 states, "Let every soul be subject to the governing authorities. For there is no authority except from God, and the authorities that exist are appointed by God. Therefore whoever resists the authority resists the ordinance of God, and those who resist will bring judgment on themselves. For rulers are not a terror to good works, but to evil." Therefore, from this verse it is clear that God Himself establishes the king's authority to govern and rule as His elect authority over the land. When we honor the authority of the king, the king appointed by God becomes a terror to evil, not a terror to good works. However, because the church has in many respects unintentionally and unknowingly dishonored the legitimate authority and full-time responsibility of the king in the kingdom business, satan has been allowed to establish strongholds in kingdom territory for which he has no right. As a sad result, I believe this is why the church possesses very little influence in the everyday affairs of our nations and our marketplace communities.

In his book *Honor's Reward*, John Bevere identifies the reason why the church can have little influence with kings in the marketplace. He states, "If the church is not perceived by our leaders as those who walk in the love and compassion of

Jesus Christ, and *true honor for their positions of authority*, they [modern-day kings] will not listen to our words [priests]."³ John Bevere even further elaborates on the importance that God Himself places on this matter by highlighting God's command in 1 Peter 2:17; "Honor all people. Love the brotherhood. Fear God. Honor the king." If the church is going to fulfill the kingdom purposes of God in our generation, we must value all people, love one another in the family of God, fear the Lord, and respect the full-time role, authority, and responsibility of the king in God's kingdom.

When Jesus walked the earth, He made a strange statement in Matthew 8:20; "Foxes have holes and birds of the air have nests, but the Son of Man has nowhere to lay His head." People think that because Jesus said He had nowhere to lay His head, it must mean that He was poor and homeless. This is not the case at all, nor does Jesus imply this with His statement. I have learned that this verse actually has nothing at all to do with poverty, but rather has everything to do with kingdom authority.

You see, in the animal kingdom, birds of the air possess domain authority in their nests. Likewise, foxes have domain authority in their holes in the ground. Now what Jesus is implying when He states that the Son of Man has nowhere to lay His head is that the domain authority of the kingdom of God, for which He is the head and which He came to restore on earth, He could not as yet give back to the sons of men on earth. You see, just as the birds possess domain authority for their nests and foxes possess domain authority for their holes, kings possesses domain authority for their kingdoms. However, until Jesus, the King of kings, had actually died on the cross and rose again, taking the keys of hell and death away from satan, He could not restore the kingdom of God to the kings of His kingdom on earth. This is why Jesus said in the same set of verses, "Follow Me, and let the dead bury their own dead" (v. 22). Until Jesus became the firstborn from the dead, His kingdom authority as the Son of Man could not be passed on or given to kings on earth who were dead to His kingdom Holy Spirit. The apostle John affirms in Revelation 1:4–5 that Jesus is the firstborn from the dead and ruler over the kings of the earth, stating, "Grace to you and peace from Him who is and who was and who is to come, and from the seven Spirits who are before His throne, and from Jesus Christ, the faithful witness, the firstborn from the dead, and the ruler over the kings of the earth."

THE RESTORATION OF THE KINGDOM OF GOD ON EARTH

To fully understand the restoration of the kingdom of God on earth, we have to go all the way back to Genesis, where it all began. In Genesis 1:26 it is recorded, "Then God said, 'Let Us make man in Our image, according to Our likeness; *let them have dominion* over the fish of the sea, over the birds of the air, and over the cattle, *over all the earth* and over every creeping thing that creeps on the earth'" (emphasis added). Notice that in this verse man was given dominion over all the earth by the explicit authority of God. Therefore, by having domain authority over the earth, man was given rulership authority of the earth as a king.

Besides giving domain authority over the earth to man, God also gave the earth to man. Psalm 115:16 records the transaction, stating, "The heaven, even the heavens, are the LORD's; But the earth He has given to the children of men." Now, we all know that if someone doesn't own something in the first place, then it is impossible for them to give it away, right? So God makes certain His Word records the rightful owner of the earth in Psalm 24:1, stating, "The earth is the LORD's, and all its fullness, The world and those who dwell therein." By these verses in the Holy Scriptures, there is no question that God had title deed to the earth and He gave it to the children of men as well as the dominion authority to rule over the earth as kings. We, therefore, have no one to blame for the current condition of the earth except ourselves.

Furthermore, we read in Genesis 1:28 that God's blessing of life included His command to man to be fruitful and multiply as well as to subdue and have dominion over the earth. With God's blessing of life, man had it real good as He walked in the authority given to him by God to establish God's kingdom rule on earth. But, unfortunately, the devil had different ideas about God's kingdom rule. So satan, in the form of a serpent, came to deceive man and steal his blessing of life as well as his kingdom authority to rule over the earth. In disobedience to God, Adam and Eve gave away the abundant blessing of life in exchange for the curse of the law of sin and death as well as forfeited to the devil their authority to subdue and have dominion on the earth. Through Adam's act of disobedience, sin and darkness was given authority to steal, kill, and destroy everything that God gave man in the Garden of Eden. Simply put, Adam and Eve lost it all—their eternal relationship with God and their kingdom authority over the earth. But praise God, the story doesn't end there.

Because God gave the authority *to man* to establish His kingdom rule on the earth and the fact that He is unable to revoke His gifts or do anything contrary to the authority of His Word, His unfailing love for man's broken condition caused

Him to leave His heavenly glorious throne and come to earth as the Son of *man*, being fully obedient even unto death on the cross, to redeem sinful man from the eternal curse of the law and deliver him from the power of darkness into the kingdom of the Son of His love, fully restoring a right standing with God, including the authority of *man* to establish God's kingdom rule on the earth in accordance with His original commandment in the Garden of Eden.

Paying the price for man's sinful disobedience with His own unblemished life, freely given unto death, Jesus—fully Son of God and fully Son of *Man*—rendered the law of sin and death completely powerless, null and void, by His blood. Therefore, what was once impossible for the unredeemed man to do is now made possible for the redeemed man of God, without limitation, through the ransomed and resurrection life of Jesus Christ living inside of us. Hence, through Jesus Christ we can once again live the abundant blessed life with God as well as fulfill the original commandment of God to establish His kingdom rule in every sphere of influence on the earth.

This is really good news in the kingdom of God because this is what it means in Matthew 18:11 when it states, "For the Son of *Man* [Jesus] has come to save that which was lost" (emphasis added). Jesus came not only to save people from their sins and restore them to a right eternal relationship with God, but also to save everything that was lost by Adam and Eve in the Garden of Eden, which included man's kingdom authority to rule over the earth as kings.

THE KINGDOM IS THE LORD'S

Psalm 22:28 declares, "For the kingdom is the LORD's, And He rules over the nations." The reason that the Lord rules over the nations is because Jesus Christ, the Son of *Man*, paid the price for the wages of sin and is now seated at the right hand of God with all authority in heaven and earth given to Him. This is affirmed by the resurrected Christ when He appeared to His disciples after His resurrection as recorded in Matthew 28:18, "And Jesus came and spoke to them, saying, 'All authority has been given to Me in heaven and on earth.'" Prior to Jesus walking the earth as a sinless *man* and paying the price of sin, satan possessed man's kingdom authority to rule over the earth. However, just as the disobedience of the one man, Adam, gave away man's kingdom authority over the earth to satan, the obedience of the one sinless man, Jesus Christ, bought back man's kingdom authority to rule over the earth.

As a result, Jesus is now seated at the right hand of God waiting till His enemies are made His footstool, as Hebrews 10:12–13 explains: "But this *Man*, after He had offered one sacrifice for sins forever, sat down at the right hand of God, from that time waiting till His enemies are made His footstool" (emphasis added). And guess who is also seated next to Him? You might not believe it, but you and I as believers in Christ are actually seated next to Him in heavenly places as joint heirs of the kingdom of God.

If you can't quite believe it, then you must read it for yourself from the Bible. Ephesians 2:4–6 states, "But God, who is rich in mercy, because of His great love with which He loved us, even when we were dead in trespasses, made us alive together with Christ (by grace you have been saved), and raised us up together, and made us sit together in the heavenly places in Christ Jesus." And Romans 8:16–17 states, "The Spirit Himself bears witness with our spirit that we are children of God, and if children, then heirs—heirs of God and joint heirs with Christ, if indeed we suffer with Him, that we may also be glorified together." So there you have it from the Word of God; we sit in heavenly places as joint heirs of the kingdom of God with Jesus Christ, our Lord, Savior, and King of kings.

And guess what is just as cool as sitting next to Him in heavenly places as joint heirs of the kingdom of God? You and I also get to play a part on earth in making the Lord's enemies His footstool and establishing His kingdom in every sphere of influence on earth. But don't fret over it, because we don't do it without any tools in our toolkit or power in our tanks. While on earth, Jesus promised His disciples that He would empower them with kingdom authority over all evil principalities and powers in wicked high places. In Matthew 16:19 the Lord states, "I will give you the keys of the kingdom of heaven, and whatever you bind on earth will be bound in heaven, and whatever you loose on earth will be loosed in heaven." And in Luke 10:19 He states, "Behold, I give you the authority to trample on serpents and scorpions, and over all the power of the enemy, and nothing shall by any means hurt you." Again, we have it clearly stated in the Word of God that we who are in Christ Jesus have been given God's kingdom authority to establish His kingdom rule on the earth, trampling upon the devil and all of his defeated wicked spiritual forces, with nothing having any means to harm us in the process.

So then the next logical question in my mind is: why don't we see more of His kingdom rule in our everyday lives in the world? Personally, I think it's because kings in Christ have, unfortunately, not fully known their kingdom rights, have not fully understood their kingdom authority, and have not fulfilled their kingdom responsibility to take the land and build the kingdom of God on earth in the power, might, and strength of the Holy Spirit. And furthermore, I think this is largely the result of church leadership being ignorant of the spiritual handcuffs that have been placed on kings by traditional church paradigms. To effectively create new paradigms of church leadership that appropriately empower kings in the kingdom business will, no doubt, require kings and priest to foster and support effective kingdom partnerships as originally intended by God when He first established the king's role in the kingdom.

5 The Kingdom Partnership

Two are better than one, Because they have a good
reward for their labor; For if they fall, one will lift
up his companion. But woe to him who is alone
when he falls; For he has no one to help him up.
Again, if two lie down together, they will keep
warm; But how can one be warm alone? Though one
may be overpowered by another, two can withstand
him. And a threefold cord is not quickly broken.
    –*Ecclesiastes 4:9–12*

KINGDOM PARTNERS FOR KINGDOM LIFE

One day while visiting New York City for a national business
conference, a colleague and I were running through Central Park
when a man ran past us wearing a T-shirt that advertised: "Will
Sell Wife for Beer." Considering that statement, I commented
to my friend that I didn't think his wife probably thought too
highly of that T-shirt. My friend laughed and said, "Yeah, his
wife probably has a T-shirt that says, 'Will Sell Husband for
Nothing.'" As we laughed about this, we could definitely imagine
how this kind of thinking certainly wouldn't make for the most
ideal marriage partnership.

At the time of writing this initial manuscript, I worked for
a very large health care system in the Gulf South. The organization is led by a chief executive officer as well as a president
and chief operating officer, with each leader having significantly

different roles and responsibilities in the organization. Because the organization is chartered as a physician-led organization, the CEO is elected by the senior physician staff members and must be a physician by training and education. Besides shaping the organization's vision and values, the CEO also leads all of the physician groups within the organization.

On the other hand, the president and COO is not a physician, nor is his position elected by the senior staff physicians. His position is rather recruited and hired by the CEO, with the primary responsibilities of the position being to lead all business and administrative aspects of the organization. In short, the CEO leads the healing functions of the company and the president leads the administrative functions of our company. Together, they form a tremendously powerful and effective partnership for achieving the organization's vision and mission.

I personally believe that the kingdom of God should be no different, possessing powerful, effective kingdom partnerships that work together to achieve the mission of the kingdom. And trust me, God believes in partnerships too. We can't get any further than twenty-six verses into the first chapter of Genesis before we see God demonstrating partnership in His kingdom: "Then God said, 'Let Us make man in Our image.'" "Let Us make" clearly means there is partnership in the Godhead.

Then again, we see God in Genesis 2:18 demonstrate His desire for man to live in a healthy partnership, declaring, "And the Lord God said, 'It is not good that man should be alone; I will make him a helper comparable to him.'" And again, we see in the New Testament Jesus promising to send us a Helper to partner with us in life, stating in John 14:16, "And I will pray the Father, and He will give you another Helper, that He may abide with you forever." By these verses and many more in the

Bible, it is clear that God designed and ordained healthy partnerships in the kingdom of God.

Furthermore, as we read Scripture, we can specifically pinpoint God's inherent design for partnership between kings and priests in the kingdom of God. In fact, the very first time we see the word *priest* in the Scriptures, it is inherently linked and embedded in the same verse as the word *king*. Genesis 14:18 records the very first time that the word *priest* is used in the Bible, "Then Melchizedek *king* of Salem brought out bread and wine; he was the *priest* of God Most High" (emphasis added). Isn't it fascinating that the first time the Bible refers to a man of God as priest, it also refers to the same man of God as king? While further study reveals that Melchizedek was a foreshadow of Jesus Christ—our perfect Priest and our perfect King—I believe the verse also points to God's implicit intent for priests and kings in the kingdom of God to be in perfect partnership together.

Plus, this is not the only verse in the Bible implying that God intends for priests and kings to be in perfect partnership in the kingdom of God. First Peter 2:9 states, "But you are a chosen generation, a *royal priesthood*, a *holy nation*, His own special people, that you may proclaim the praises of Him who called you out of darkness into His marvelous light" (emphasis added). Notice the order and placement of all the words in this verse—it is certainly not by accident or by coincidence.

With the words *royal priesthood*, let me ask, who is royalty reserved for and who is the priesthood reserved for? Of course, we all know that royalty is reserved for kings and the priesthood is reserved for priests. With God placing the word *royal* ahead of the word *priesthood*, it would appear that God is placing a higher value on the role of the king over the role of the priest, right? Well, not so fast!

I marvel at how God completely reverses the order and placement of the next two words—*holy nation*—in the very same verse. Now with the words *holy nation*, let me ask: What role in the kingdom is ascribed as being holy and what role in the kingdom is ascribed to ruling a nation? Again, we of course all know that priests are to be holy and kings are to rule nations. Seemingly, by the order and placement of these two words, it would appear that God is now placing a higher value on the role of the priest over the role of the king, right? However, by reversing the order and placement of these two words in the very same verse, "royal priesthood, holy nation," I believe God is actually saying that neither the role of priest or king carries more value or importance than the other to Him in His kingdom. In short, I believe a "royal priesthood" of kings and priests and a "holy nation" of priests and kings simply implies a two-way equal kingdom partnership between kings and priests, and priests and kings:

- Royal...Priesthood   Holy...Nation
- Kings and Priests   Priests and Kings
- Two-Way   Equal Partnership

THE SEPARATION OF
CHURCH AND STATE KINGDOM DIVIDE

While God has said that His kingdom is a royal priesthood, a holy nation, a two-way equal partnership of kings and priests, I believe that America's separation of church and state mentality has actually infiltrated church thinking and, unfortunately, allowed the devil to cunningly divide God's intended kingdom partnership. In Mark 10:9, addressing a group of Pharisees who were testing Jesus regarding the marriage partnership between a husband and wife, Jesus explicitly states, "Therefore what God has joined together, let not man separate." Now I know that this may be a radical statement for some people in the church as well as some people in the state, but I believe that God never intended for man to separate His kingdom partnership of kings and priests. In fact, in Luke 11:17, once again addressing erroneous thinking from the Pharisees, Jesus explicitly teaches them, "Every kingdom divided against itself is brought to desolation, and a house divided against a house falls."

In this context, Jesus was making a point that if He was casting out devils by the power of the devil, then how could the devil's kingdom stand? Therefore, if the devil's kingdom cannot stand if it is divided, what makes us think that the kingdom of God can stand if it is divided? Unfortunately, the kingdom of God today is in all practicality divided because the real kingdom partnership of kings and priests has been separated by a separation of church and state mentality. However, in stating this, please understand that I am in no way advocating a commingling of separate powers between church and state offices nor am I recommending a commingling of separate powers between the offices of priest and king in the kingdom of God. There is definite wisdom in the separation of the powers of office between church and state as well as priest and king—different roles, different functions, different powers, but the same kingdom of God.

However, because of the church's subtle embrace of America's separation of church and state mentality, the royal priesthood, holy nation, perfect kingdom partnership between kings and priests originally intended by God is slowly being *subverted* into a *royal nation, holy priesthood*, divided kingdom partnership between kings and priests. And if you honestly look at the kingdom of God in America today, for the most part, priests are separately pursuing their God-ordained purposes in nonprofit ministry and kings are attempting to separately pursue their God-ordained purposes in for-profit kingdom ventures, while the two purposes never really come together in effective *spiritual* kingdom partnership. The real problem with this spiritual separation in the kingdom of God is that it opens the door for the enemy to split the kingdom in two with kings on one side—a royal nation—and priests on the other—a holy priesthood—which God never intended for His own special people. I believe that God expects His kings and priests to *spiritually* partner together as His kingdom dream team better than we are currently doing today.

If you don't think so, let me share the real-life testimony of Hans and Dani Johnson—kings in the kingdom of God feeling the despair that results when priests and kings are not working effectively together in kingdom partnership as God originally intended. The following written testimony is taken directly from Dani's book entitled *Spirit Driven Success*, endorsed by The Make It Happen Learning Institute as a Make It Happen Book™. In her book, she states the following:

> Let me tell you something. There is no disconnect between God and the marketplace. There is no disconnect between God and what you do for a living. In fact, in Colossians 3:23 we are told "And whatsoever ye do, do it heartily, as to the Lord, and not unto men." That's what it says. This is only one of the many business references found in the Bible.
>
> My husband and I once felt that disconnect too. We struggled to find our place and felt like total failures in the body of Christ. We felt that we weren't being used. We were going to our pastor and telling him what we

could do and asking, "Can you use us?" Over and over we were told, "Ah, not right now. Maybe some day."

We had helped thousands of people in the marketplace make ridiculous income, healed marriages and restored families. Yet, when we presented this saying, "Here's what we do and we'd like to help," we simply heard, "Why don't you volunteer?"

So, for years we felt useless in the Body of Christ. What could we do for God? We didn't fit into the "traditional" structure of the church and felt we were not accepted for what we wanted to give.

Some day never came for us. Year after year, after year, we kept feeling hopeless and useless sitting in the pews paying our tithes.[1]

I believe that Hans and Dani Johnson aren't the only kings in the kingdom who feel the pain of being marginalized in the kingdom of God. In fact, I think we would be surprised by the number of kings in the kingdom feeling this exact same way, but they keep silent about it because they don't know how to express it or possibly fear a spirit of religion in their churches. As a result, they just keep silently thinking that no one really cares about their gifts and talents in the marketplace. Or worse, feeling useless to the church, they just stop going to church, all the while still having the same question pounding in their heart and mind: "Do I have purpose in the kingdom of God and does my everyday work matter to His kingdom?" I believe that the Holy Spirit has revealed to me that God is going to not only answer those questions for the kings in the kingdom but also use them mightily to build His kingdom on earth in these last days.

THE PROFIT VS. NONPROFIT KINGDOM DIVIDE

But unfortunately, there is an additional separation issue in the kingdom of God, which I think is further contributing to a subtle spiritual split between kings and priests. Somehow over time, I believe that we have embraced spiritual division in the kingdom of God along the lines of for-profit corporate tax structures and nonprofit corporate tax structures. Because of the community benefit requirement for nonprofit tax status in America, I think the nonprofit tax status of the church has become viewed as an indicator of a greater-valued work in the kingdom of God as compared to the kingdom work of for-profit tax status organizations in the business community. Unfortunately, this kind of thinking creates two different class distinctions in the kingdom of God around an organization's tax structure, which God is totally indifferent about. Regardless of corporate tax structure, God cares intently about all kingdom work in His kingdom—taxed or not.

In fact, when challenged by the Pharisees about paying taxes, Jesus is recorded in Matthew 22:21 as saying, "Render therefore to Caesar the things that are Caesar's, and to God the things that are God's." In essence, Jesus was telling the Pharisees that paying taxes to the government was not the issue that needed to be addressed; it was rather a heart issue about money and authority that really needed to be addressed. After 2,000 years, nothing has changed—we give to Caesar what belongs to Caesar and we give to God what belongs to God. Our corporate tax structures simply do not matter to God when it comes to His kingdom purposes because He owns all the money in the kingdom anyway. Haggai 2:8 declares, "'The silver is Mine, and the gold is Mine,' says the LORD of hosts."

In Scripture, Jesus affirms that the Lord is Lord over all,

including taxes, when He and Peter were approached by temple tax collectors as recorded in Matthew 17:24–27:

> When they had come to Capernaum, those who received the temple tax came to Peter and said, "Does your Teacher not pay the temple tax?" He said, "Yes." And when he had come into the house, Jesus anticipated him, saying, "What do you think, Simon? From whom do the kings of the earth take customs or taxes, from their sons or from strangers?" Peter said to Him, "From strangers." Jesus said to him, "Then the sons are free. Nevertheless, lest we offend them, go to the sea, cast in a hook, and take the fish that comes up first. And when you have opened its mouth, you will find a piece of money; take that and give it to them for Me and you."

From these passages it is clear to me that Jesus does in fact support a tax-exempt benefit for our churches, specifically emphasizing His illustrated point to Peter that the sons of the king do not pay taxes. In fact, I wouldn't doubt that the intent of our country's tax laws for nonprofit tax status have their origin in these specific scripture verses in Matthew. Therefore, without question, I believe our country should continue to uphold the nonprofit tax benefit for our churches as well as other nonprofit organizations that benefit our communities. We are a far better nation with far better communities in our own nation as well as around the world because of the tax-exempt privileges granted to appropriately qualifying nonprofit organizations in America.

With my unequivocal full support for the privileges afforded our tax-exempt organizations in America, the point I am making in this matter is not about laws of taxation. The point is rather that the value of work done in the kingdom of God is not determined by tax status in the eyes of God and should not be a barrier to spiritual kingdom partnership between kings and priests in the advancement of God's kingdom purposes on earth. Because it is God's will that His kingdom come on earth as it is in heaven, God rather determines the value of His kingdom work by the work done as fishers of men for the kingdom of God in any capacity—tax-exempt or not. By Jesus' direction to Peter in the applicable verses of Matthew 17 to go fishing and open the mouth of the first fish he caught to find money for the payment of the taxes, I believe the Lord is demonstrating that (1) the primary focus of the kingdom is fishing for men, regardless of tax status and (2) there is no reason to be offensive over the matter of taxation, because God is Jehovah Jireh, the Lord our Provider, including the Provider for our taxes. And lastly, when Jesus told Peter, "Take the money and give it to them for Me and you," I believe the Lord was demonstrating His honor for God's intended kingdom partnership between kings and priests.

However, because nonprofit church organizations in America are believed to be doing God's highest-value work by virtue of their nonprofit tax status, many people think that the for-profit work of business organizations actually has less value and purpose in the kingdom of God. This kind of thinking actually puts limitations on God and creates subtle division in His kingdom along the lines of tax status. Personally, I think this kind of thinking has some roots in misinterpreting the parable of the rich young ruler and teaching that God thinks negatively about the wealth obtained and possessed by him. Furthermore, correlating such teaching with Mark 8:36—"For what will it profit a man if he gains the whole world, and loses his own soul?"—unfortunately creates a "perfect storm" religious mindset that God has a disdain for profit-making work in the kingdom of God, which simply isn't true when the full context of Scripture is taken into account.

As emphasized earlier in this chapter, the Bible affirms that whatever work we do matters to God and has value in the kingdom; otherwise, there would be no reward of the inheritance from the Lord for doing it as unto Him. Colossians 3:23–24 states, "And whatever you do, do it heartily, as to the Lord and not to men, knowing that from the Lord you will receive the reward of the inheritance; for you serve the Lord Christ." Have no misunderstanding about it, your work and purpose as a king in the marketplace really do matter to God and do have eternal value in the kingdom.

THE RICH YOUNG RULER'S KEY TO THE KINGDOM

So then, regarding the rich young ruler; if Jesus wasn't teaching about His dislike for wealth and riches, what did He mean when He said that it would be easier for a camel to fit through the eye of a needle than it would be for a rich man to enter the kingdom of God? This is a great question, but to adequately answer it we have to understand the full context of the rich young ruler's encounter with Jesus found in Matthew 19:16–24:

> Now behold, one came [to Jesus] and said to Him, "Good Teacher, what good thing shall I do that I may have eternal life?" So He said to him, "Why do you call Me good? No one is good but One, that is, God. But if you want to enter into life, keep the commandments." He said to Him, "Which ones?" Jesus said, "'You shall not murder,' 'You shall not commit adultery,' 'You shall not steal,' 'You shall not bear false witness,' 'Honor your father and your mother,' and, 'You shall love your neighbor as yourself.' The young man said to Him, "All

these things I have kept from my youth. What do I still lack?" Jesus said to him, "If you want to be perfect, go, sell what you have and give to the poor, and you will have treasure in heaven; and come, follow Me." But when the young man heard that saying, he went away sorrowful, for he had great possessions.

Then Jesus said to His disciples, "Assuredly, I say to you that it is hard for a rich man to enter the kingdom of heaven. And again I say to you, it is easier for a camel to go through the eye of a needle than for a rich man to enter the kingdom of God."

THE PERFECT KINGDOM OF GOD REVEALED

Let me carefully breakdown this encounter with Jesus so that you can understand its full meaning. First of all, we must understand that this encounter is not about God's dislike for rich young rulers. It's really about the perfect kingdom of God and His total compassion for the rich young ruler and his potential destiny in the kingdom of God.

To begin with, when Jesus asked the rich young ruler, "Why do you call me good?" He is actually testing the young man to see if he knows who He really is. Jesus isn't just some good ole rabbi teacher; He is actually God Most High—the One who is perfect Priest and perfect King over God's perfect kingdom, just like Melchizedek who was priest and king over Salem. In this complete exchange with the rich young ruler, Jesus is actually revealing to us that He is the perfect Melchizedek of the perfect kingdom of God.

As perfect Priest, Jesus first addresses the matter of salvation in this young man's life by stating that if he wants to enter into life, he must first keep the commandments of the Book of the Law, knowing full well that everyone, including the rich young ruler, has transgressed the Law of God and is in need of a Savior. So Jesus, our perfect Priest, is taking care of first things first in expressing His concern for the young man's eternal life and his need for personal salvation to enter the kingdom of God. Unfortunately, at that moment the rich young ruler was deceived and spiritually blind to his need for a Savior, thinking that he was already good enough to enter the kingdom of God without a personal Savior.

Secondly, as perfect King, Jesus begins to share kingdom principles with the rich young ruler; but again, as a result of being dead to sin without the salvation of God shed in his heart, he was spiritually blind to the kingdom principles that Jesus was sharing with him about real wealth and riches in the kingdom of God. You see, when Jesus told the rich young ruler to go and sell his possessions and give the money to the poor, it's not because Jesus had some problem with him having wealth and possessions. It's actually just the opposite, because Jesus was in fact giving him the key to having real wealth and possessions in the kingdom of God. The key is found in Luke 6:38: "Give, and it will be given to you: good measure, pressed down, shaken together, and running over will be put into your bosom. For with the same measure that you use, it will be measured back to you." Simply put, Jesus wasn't trying to take away the rich young ruler's wealth; He was rather teaching the rich young ruler how to gain real wealth and possessions in the kingdom of God: by seeking first His kingdom and giving generously to others.

So perhaps you are thinking, *But what about the camel and the eye of the needle statement?* Let me explain further what I have learned about this parable. In ancient times, people would travel far distances on camels to get to wherever they were going. After a long journey, they would need to wash off the dust and grime from their camels. To do this, they would put their camels through a narrow, tight place that would allow them to grasp the camel firmly and effectively wash them off. So, I guess you could say the eye of the camel's needle was the world's very first car wash. But seriously, this really is how the camel owners of that day would actually wash their camels after long journeys.

Now the point of Jesus using this specific illustration, stating that "it is easier for a camel to go through the eye of a needle than for a rich man to enter the kingdom of God" is to actually point out how difficult it is for someone who has achieved wealth and possessions outside of the kingdom of God to part with their ways for obtaining them and fully embrace God's narrow kingdom way that will not only lead to wealth and riches in the kingdom of God, but also lead to eternal life in His kingdom. Just like the camel being washed through the narrow eye of the needle, young rich rulers by the world's standards must wash off the dirt and grime of their journey to obtain wealth and possessions by forgetting their common worldly ways and renewing their minds to God's uncommon paradoxical kingdom ways: Give and you shall receive, lose your life and you will gain it, be a servant of all and you will be the greatest. While these paradoxical spiritual principles may not make sense to the natural human mind in the common world, they do make perfect sense to the supernatural mind of Christ in God's uncommon perfect kingdom.

And by the way, did you happen to notice the perfect kingdom partnership at work in Jesus' encounter with the rich young ruler? The perfect Priest sharing the person of Jesus and the perfect King sharing the principles of Jesus—two roles, two purposes, same kingdom. In essence, I believe the perfect Priest in Jesus was communicating Psalm 37:4, "Delight yourself in the

LORD [the person of Jesus], And He shall give you the desires of your heart," and the perfect King in Him was communicating Matthew 6:33, "But seek first the kingdom of God and His righteousness [the principles of Jesus], and all these things shall be added to you." This is certainly something for kings and priests to think about as we spiritually partner together to save souls and build the kingdom of God on earth as it is in heaven.

TRUE KINGDOM PARTNERSHIP IS A PARTNERSHIP OF THE LIVING WORD

Before closing this chapter, I'd like to share with you a biblical picture of a healthy partnership between kings and priests found in 2 Chronicles 17:6–10. Speaking of King Jehoshaphat's reign, the Bible records his righteous ways:

> And his heart took delight in the ways of the LORD; moreover he removed the high places and wooden images from Judah. Also in the third year of his reign he sent his leaders [ambassadors of the king], Ben-Hail, Obadiah, Zechariah, Nethanel, and Michaiah, to teach in the cities of Judah. And with them he sent Levites: Shemaiah, Nethaniah, Zebadiah, Asahel, Shemiramoth, Jehonathan, Adonijah, Tobijah, and Tobadonijah—the Levites [ambassadors of the priest]; and with them Elishama and Jehoram, the priests. So they taught in Judah, and had the Book of the Law of the LORD with them; they went throughout all the cities of Judah and taught the people. And the fear of the LORD fell on all the kingdoms of the lands that were around Judah, so that they did not make war against Jehoshaphat.

Do you see the picture of God's perfect kingdom partnership between kings and priests at work in these verses? Kings and priests were sent as partners throughout all of the cities sharing with people the Book of the Law and teaching them the principles of the kingdom of God. In so doing, the kingdom enjoyed great influence in the world because the fear of the Lord fell upon all the kingdoms of the lands surrounding them.

It is the same exact thing that Jesus was doing when He encountered the rich young ruler. As perfect Priest, He taught the Book of the Law, pointing to the need for a Savior. As perfect King, He taught the principles of the kingdom, pointing to the abundant life found in kingdom living. The result is a powerful, perfect kingdom partnership that saves souls, heals people, takes ground, builds the kingdom, and makes disciples of every tribe, nation, and tongue as commanded by the Lord in Matthew 28:19–20: "Go therefore and make disciples of all the nations, baptizing them in the name of the Father and of the Son and of the Holy Spirit, teaching them to observe all things that I have commanded you; and lo, I am with you always, even to the end of the age."

When priests and kings of the kingdom of God work in full partnership to honor each other's role and function in the kingdom, they form a perfect kingdom partnership as God intends. And as a result, the kingdom of God will not only save souls into the kingdom, but also possess great influence in every sphere of influence around the world.

6 The Restoration of Kings to the Kingdom Business

The LORD did not set His love on you nor choose
you because you were more in number than any
other people, for you were the least of all peoples;
but because the LORD loves you, and because
He would keep the oath which He swore to your
fathers, the LORD has brought you out with a
mighty hand, and redeemed you from the house
of bondage, from the hand of Pharaoh king of
Egypt. Therefore know that the LORD your God,
He is God, the faithful God who keeps covenant
and mercy for a thousand generations with those
who love Him and keep His commandments.
—Deuteronomy 7:7–9

THE WITHERED HAND REVELATION

Not long ago the Lord led me to go on a business men's missions
trip to Potchefstroom, South Africa, with eight other business
men and my executive pastor. In preparation for the trip, I spent
five days fasting and praying that God's plans and purposes for
the trip would be accomplished through our missions team.
One morning while we were there, I was up very early praying
and seeking God. As I was reading, the Lord led me to the
passages of Scripture found in Matthew 12:9–14, where Jesus
heals a man's withered hand on the Sabbath.

Now when He [Jesus] had departed from there, He went into their synagogue. And behold, there was a man who had a withered hand. And they asked Him, saying, "Is it lawful to heal on the Sabbath?"—that they might accuse Him. Then He said to them, "What man is there among you who has one sheep, and if it falls into a pit on the Sabbath, will not lay hold of it and lift it out? Of how much more value then is a man than a sheep? Therefore it is lawful to do good on the Sabbath." Then He said to the man, "Stretch out your hand." And he stretched it out, and *it was restored as whole as the other.* Then the Pharisees went out and plotted against Him, how they might destroy Him.

—EMPHASIS ADDED

As I was reading these verses, the verse that says the Lord restored the man's hand as whole as the other hand kept jumping out at me with inner intrigue. So I began to ask the Lord some questions about this whole encounter with the Pharisees and the man with a withered hand.

Lord, why did You heal the man's withered hand and specifically state that You restored it as whole as the other hand? What's the purpose of the hands and what meaning do they have in this encounter with the Pharisees on the Sabbath?

Then in a small, soft, inner voice, the Lord began to speak to me and answer my questions, saying, "The hands represent two purposes in the kingdom of God—the purpose to heal and the purpose to build; however, neither purpose is worthy of the kingdom unless it is accomplished through the nail-pierced hands of the Cross. The whole hand is the hand that represents the healing hand of the priests in the kingdom which is well-functioning in its kingdom purpose; however, the withered hand represents the building hand of the kings in the kingdom which is currently withered and malfunctioning in its kingdom purpose."

He then went on to tell me that when He walked the earth, He went about laying hands on people as a Priest, healing them of all of their sin, sickness, and disease, but He also used His hands on earth as a carpenter King, building the kingdom of God in everyday spheres of marketplace influence. He then emphasized to me that the kingdom of God is designed to be a healthy partnership of priests and kings, but that the partnership was currently not working as designed. And because of it, He told me that He was going to restore the withered hand of the kings in the kingdom as whole as the hand of the priests in the kingdom so that His kingdom on earth could be properly built in everyday spheres of influence through a healthy kingdom partnership between His kings and His priests.

And with that powerful revelation, the Lord began to put together all of the parts and pieces of teaching and revelation that He has shared with me over the last five years, including the teachings that I've heard and learned from anointed pastors and apostles, writing the entire context of this book in my heart as His message to the kings and priests of His kingdom on earth today. As such, I am only writing this book because the Lord has called me to be His messenger and I am being faithful to deliver His message to inspire His kings to come forth and begin building the Lord's kingdom in the marketplace through a healthy kingdom partnership with His priests. As my senior pastor would say, "I'm just God's pizza delivery boy." I'm only responsible for delivering the pizza. It's your responsibility to appropriately respond as the Lord leads and guides you.

THE KING'S REIGN IN PURPOSEFUL
WORK ON EARTH

In Proverbs 8:15–16 the Lord declares, "By Me kings reign, And rulers decree justice. By Me princes rule, and nobles, All the judges of the earth." By this declaration of Scripture, we can rest assured that there isn't a single leader on the face of the earth who God has not put into office, nor given the authority to lead in his or her position. While the United States of America is the greatest democratic free society in the world, make no mistake about it, each elected president has been and will always be hand-picked by almighty God Himself, ensuring that His ultimate will and purpose for the United States will be done in the earth. Proverbs 21:1 (NLT) states, "The king's heart is like a stream of water directed by the LORD; he guides it wherever he pleases." And the same goes for all other leaders of the nations of the world, democratic or not, as well as every leader at every level in every organization—they reign, rule, and decree justice by God's sovereign authority so that His will is ultimately accomplished, no matter what.

The apostle Paul affirms God's sovereign authority in Romans 13:1, stating, "Let every soul be subject to the governing authorities. For there is no authority except from God, and the authorities that exist are appointed by God." Even Jesus powerfully affirmed this truth when He was brought before Pilate on false charges as recorded in John 19:10–11: "Then Pilate said to Him, 'Are You not speaking to me? Do You not know that I have power to crucify You, and power to release You?' Jesus answered, 'You could have no power at all against Me unless it had been given you from above.'" Therefore, it is very clear from the Scriptures that God grants the authority and the power to every leader to lead in his or her position. With that said, it shouldn't be too hard to believe that our work as kings in the kingdom certainly does matter to God; otherwise, why would He grant us the authority and power to lead in our roles?

As touched upon in the previous chapter, there is unfortunately a tendency for the church to look upon the temporal work of kings to meet the everyday needs of people on earth as having less value than the eternal work of priests to meet the salvation needs of people in everlasting glory. However, the work that kings do on earth to help meet the needs of the Lord's creation has every bit as much value and importance to God as does the work that priests do to meet the salvation needs of the Lord's creation in everlasting glory.

Doug Sherman and William Hendricks help to answer the question "What really counts?" in the following excerpt taken from their book entitled, *Your Work Matters To God*:

> This is all well and good, the missionary might respond. It's true that [making] drill presses may have great value in time. But don't we want to give our lives to things that will have great value in eternity? If I lead some person to salvation in Christ, I'll be able to look on the fruit of my labor for the rest of eternity. But the architect who puts up a building must someday watch that building pass away. And in eternity he'll have little if anything to show for his earthy labor. Wouldn't he rather give his life to what really counts?
>
> But I would reply that he actually is giving his life to what "really counts"—what counts both in eternity and in time. What will ultimately matter in eternity is our faithfulness right now with the resources and responsibilities God has given us.
>
> So the architect who designs buildings to the glory of God, who works with integrity, diligence, fairness,

and excellence, who treats his wife with the love Christ has for the Church, who raises his children in godly wisdom and instruction, who urges non-Christian coworkers and associates to heed the gospel message— in short, who acts as a responsible manager in the various arenas God has entrusted to him—this man will receive eternal praise from God. That is what really matters in eternity.

In time, meanwhile, what "really matters" to God is that the various needs of His creation be met. One of those needs is the salvation of people, and for that He sent Christ to die and He sends the Church to tell the world about what Christ did.

But in addition to salvation—obviously a need with eternal implications—mankind has many other [temporal] needs.[1]

Again, in the excerpt you just read, can you see the perfect kingdom partnership of kings and priests at work in the kingdom of God to meet the *temporal* and *eternal* needs of God's creation on earth? However, if kings are not valued in the work they do to meet the temporal needs of God's creation to the same degree that priests are valued in the work they do to meet the eternal needs of God's creation, the temporal and eternal kingdom of God suffers a distorted value of kingdom work, which was perfectly designed by God to meet all of His creation's legitimate needs—whether temporal or eternal. This can only be remedied through a spirit of truth and grace that leads to unity within the body of Christ to honor and respect the value of everyone's kingdom assignments given by God to meet the legitimate needs of His most valued creation—that is, people.

First Chronicles 27:25–31 records the kingdom assignments

of King David's leaders to meet the legitimate needs of God's people in the kingdom of Israel.

> And Azmaveth the son of Adiel was over the king's treasuries; and Jehonathan the son of Uzziah was over the storehouses in the field, in the cities, in the villages, and in the fortresses. Ezri the son of Chelub was over those who did the work of the field for tilling the ground. And Shimei the Ramathite was over the vineyards, and Zabdi the Shiphmite was over the produce of the vineyards for the supply of wine. Baal-Hanan the Gederite was over the olive trees and the sycamore trees that were in the lowlands, and Joash was over the store of oil. And Shitrai the Sharonite was over the herds that fed in Sharon, and Shaphat the son of Adlai was over the herds that were in the valleys. Obil the Ishmaelite was over the camels, Jehdeiah the Meronothite was over the donkeys, and Jaziz the Hagrite was over the flocks. All these were the officials over King David's property.

Each of these leadership assignments served a significant purpose in the kingdom of Israel. In the very same way, each of our leadership assignments on earth today serves a significant purpose in the kingdom of God and carries with it great power and responsibility to influence the world for His glory and His honor.

GREAT POWER CARRIES GREAT RESPONSIBILITY

By God's design, kings have influence in our world to transform society because God gave them power to have dominion, even dominion over the works of His hands. The Bible declares in Psalm 8:4–9:

What is man that You are mindful of him, And the
son of man that You visit him? For You have made him
a little lower than the angels, And You have crowned
him with glory and honor. You have made him to have
dominion over the works of Your hands; You have put
all things under his feet, All sheep and oxen—Even
the beasts of the field, The birds of the air, And the
fish of the sea That pass through the paths of the seas.
O LORD, our Lord, How excellent is Your name in all
the earth!

If you meditate on that truth for too long, it will certainly
deepen within you a healthy fear of the Lord.

In this Psalm, the psalmist is reminding us of God's original
intent in the Garden of Eden for man to be fruitful, multiply,
subdue, and have kingdom dominion over the earth. God desires
this so much for man that He even made man to have dominion
over the works of His very own hands. Do you realize how
much responsibility that this kind of dominion power carries
for the Lord's kingdom ambassadors on earth?

In the movie *Spider-Man*®, released in 2002, Peter Parker
fully realizes the immense power that has been gifted to him
as Spider-Man and discusses it with his Uncle Ben. Peter's
Uncle Ben shares this tremendous insight about power: "With
great power comes great responsibility."[2] As the Lord's kingdom
ambassadors on earth, I think Uncle Ben's insight is most
certainly worthy of thoughtful actions to be responsible kings
in the kingdom of God. In so doing, we will possess tremendous
leadership influence to shape the state of affairs in our nations
and our communities.

In essence, through God's original blessing in the Garden
of Eden and the restoration of that blessing through the blood

of Christ at Calvary, God has given His kingdom ambassadors on earth the power to transform societies for His glory and His honor. But whether or not kings in the kingdom of God choose to use that great power appropriately and as God intends is entirely a matter of great responsibility and choice. Unfortunately, history has shown that kings don't always make the right choices in living up to the level of great responsibility that their great power demands.

The Book of Kings records many instances of great failures of the kings of Israel to appropriately use their power and leadership influence to impact the nation of Israel for God's glory and honor. As a result, the nation and the people suffered the consequences of their kings' poor choices and lack of responsibility to God and the people they were serving. The following is a *Reader's Digest* list of Israel's kings who can be counted in the number who did evil in the sight of the Lord:

1. King Solomon—1 Kings 11:6

2. King Jeroboam—1 Kings 15:3

3. King Nadab—1 Kings 15:26

4. King Basha—1 Kings 15:34

5. King Omri—1 Kings 16:25

6. King Ahab—1 Kings 16:30

7. King Ahaziah (son of Ahab)—1 Kings 22:52

8. King Jehoram—2 Kings 3:2

9. King Ahaziah (son of Jehoram)—2 Kings 8:27

10. King Jehoahaz—2 Kings 13:2

11. King Jehoash—2 Kings 13:11

12. King Jeroboam—2 Kings 14:24
13. King Zechariah—2 Kings 15:9
14. King Menahem—2 Kings 15:18
15. King Pekahiah—2 Kings 15:24
16. King Pekah—2 Kings 15:28
17. King Hoshea—2 Kings 17:2
18. King Manasseh—2 Kings 21:2
19. King Amon—2 Kings 21:20
20. King Jehoahaz—2 Kings 23:32
21. King Jehoiakim—2 Kings 23:37
22. King Jehoiachim—2 Kings 24:9
23. King Zedekiah—2 Kings 24:19

As you can see from this long list of kings in Israel's history who did not appropriately handle their great power by doing evil in the sight of the Lord, it is clear that kings can possess a wicked propensity to allow their great power to corrupt them greatly in the eyes of God, with devastating results to the kingdom. Sadly the Bible records in 1 Kings 11:4 that King Solomon, the wisest king that ever lived, divided his heart toward God: "For it was so, when Solomon was old, that his wives turned his heart after other gods; and his heart was not loyal to the LORD his God, as was the heart of his father David." As a result, King Solomon's divided heart left behind a legacy of a divided kingdom—the kingdom of Israel and the kingdom of Judah—which were both eventually dissolved in captivity and deportation to other nations.

Unfortunately, it's still the same today. If not careful to

maintain a healthy fear of the Lord, kings can abuse and misappropriate the dominion authority that God has given them. As a result, God's kingdom on earth can be divided in wickedness, lacking any real power to transform our society for His kingdom and His glory.

The King's Power Under Control

In Daniel 4:28–37 (The Message), the Bible records how the powerful hand of God can humble a king as well as how the grace of God can restore a fallen king to his kingdom, making it better than ever.

> All this happened to King Nebuchadnezzar. Just twelve months later, he was walking on the balcony of the royal palace in Babylon and boasted, "Look at this, Babylon the great! And I built it all by myself, a royal palace adequate to display my honor and glory!" The words were no sooner out of his mouth than a voice out of heaven spoke, "This is the verdict on you, King Nebuchadnezzar: Your kingdom is taken from you. You will be driven out of human company and live with the wild animals. You will eat grass like an ox. The sentence is for seven seasons, enough time to learn that the High God rules human kingdoms and puts whomever he wishes in charge." It happened at once. Nebuchadnezzar was driven out of human company, ate grass like an ox, and was soaked in heaven's dew. His hair grew like the feathers of an eagle and his nails like the claws of a hawk. At the end of the seven years, I, Nebuchadnezzar, looked to heaven. I was given my mind back and I blessed the High God, thanking and glorifying God, who lives forever. "His sovereign rule lasts and lasts, his kingdom never declines and falls.

Life on this earth doesn't add up to much, but God's heavenly army keeps everything going. No one can interrupt His work, no one can call His rule into question." At the same time that I was given back my mind, I was also given back my majesty and splendor, making my kingdom shine. All the leaders and important people came looking for me. I was reestablished as king in my kingdom and became greater than ever. And that's why I'm singing—I, Nebuchadnezzar—singing and praising the King of Heaven: "Everything He does is right, and He does it the right way. He knows how to turn a proud person into a humble man or woman."

The recorded biblical account of King Nebuchadnezzer should serve as a wake-up call to the kings of this earth that pride is an offense to almighty God, leading to His merciful correction under His mighty hand. As kings in the Lord's kingdom that lasts and lasts and never declines and falls, we are His ambassadors on earth to make His kingdom shine in every sphere of influence that He has given us.

If, in the process of fulfilling our kingdom roles as kings, we allow pride to creep into our hearts and deceive us into thinking that our role is higher than God's role in building His kingdom, we can rest assured that we will fall and be corrected as was King Nebuchadnezzar. In this matter, Proverbs 16:18–19 offers wise counsel, stating, "Pride goes before destruction, And a haughty spirit before a fall. Better to be of a humble spirit with the lowly, Than to divide the spoil with the proud." Because God gives kings the power to influence and build, we must carefully guard our hearts from the sin of prideful thinking by carefully surrounding ourselves with wise, humble people and submitting ourselves to our elders in God, who care for us in the same way that God cares for us.

Peter affirms the wisdom in humbly submitting ourselves to the spiritual authority in our lives, stating in 1 Peter 5:5–7, "Likewise you younger people, submit yourselves to your elders. Yes, all of you be submissive to one another, and be clothed with humility, for 'God resists the proud, But gives grace to the humble.' Therefore humble yourselves under the mighty hand of God, that He may exalt you in due time, casting all your care upon Him, for He cares for you."

I once heard one of my pastors comment that the scariest thing about a deceived person is that they don't know that they are deceived. If you think about it, that really is a scary thought, which is why kings must have priests who love God and people enough to risk the people's approval and courageously speak the truth in love.

I also find that parables and illustrations help us to discover truth about ourselves by shedding light in the potentially dark places of our hearts and minds. Because kings have power, pride can so cleverly mask itself in the psyche of a king without him clearly seeing it. Therefore, I offer this illustration regarding the power of an elephant to help shed light on the difference between a king with pride and a king with humility. You see, all elephants, like kings, have tremendous power. An elephant under control, such as a trained elephant in the circus, possesses tremendous power, but because it is controlled by the ringmaster, the elephant's power can be harnessed for doing good. However, a wild, untrained elephant out of control also possesses tremendous power, but without a ringmaster to train it to be under control, its unchecked power can do major destruction and inflict serious harm.

Kings are just like these two elephants. Kings who invite the Holy Spirit to be their "ringmaster" learn to develop self-control and harness their power for doing good. Kings who do not invite the Holy Spirit to be their ringmaster only operate from their flesh, never learning to develop real self-control, and unfortunately, can often use their power to do great harm to themselves and to others. I implore and encourage all kings to invite the Holy Spirit to be the ringmaster of your life every day of your life so that the power you have as a king may be harnessed by the Holy Spirit to do massive good in His kingdom.

The king who humbles himself under the mighty hand of the Lord is the king who has true power and real influence. In his book of leadership quotes entitled, *The Power of Leadership*, John Maxwell states, "Leadership is influence."[3] Additionally, the apostle Ron Carpenter of Redemption World Outreach Ministries teaches that the definition of the word *responsibility* simply means the ability to respond. Therefore, as kings in the kingdom, we possess great power through the ability to respond to our world in ways that will either influence it for good or for evil. This is why we must be careful to live in obedience to the Lord our God just like King Jotham is recorded as having done in 2 Chronicles 27:6 (NLT), "King Jotham became powerful because he was careful to live in obedience to the LORD his God."

When we live in obedience to the Lord as kings in the kingdom, we gain His power in Christ to completely transform modern-day society for His kingdom and His glory. The magnitude of this power and responsibility is simply too much for a person to fully comprehend without having the mind of Christ to reveal its potential impact on earth. "O LORD, our Lord, How excellent is Your name in all the earth!" (Ps. 8:9).

7 The Awakened Kingdom Mandate

All the kings of the earth shall praise You,
O LORD, When they hear the words of Your
mouth. Yes, they shall sing of the ways of the
LORD, For great is the glory of the LORD.
—*Psalm 138:4–5*

THE KING'S CROWN OF GLORY

In the twelfth chapter of the Book of John, there is a remarkable story recorded about Mary, the sister of Lazarus, which I believe has significant relevance to kings in the marketplace. In verses 1–3, it is recorded, "Then, six days before the Passover, Jesus came to Bethany, where Lazarus was who had been dead, whom He had raised from the dead. There they made Him a supper; and Martha served, but Lazarus was one of those who sat at the table with Him. Then Mary took a pound of very costly oil of spikenard, anointed the feet of Jesus, and wiped His feet with her hair. And the house was filled with the fragrance of the oil."

The reason I believe this story is so significant to kings working in the business marketplace is that the spikenard oil that Mary used to anoint the feet of Jesus was so expensive that it was worth one year of a person's wages at that time. I believe that because the oil was worth a year's salary, it actually could serve to represent a king's full year of work which could be done as worthy worship unto the Lord. Additionally, because Mary used her hair to wipe the Lord's feet, she was actually taking her hair, the glory of a woman, and laying it at the Lord's feet in thankfulness for the freedom and peace that He brought to her life. Isaiah 52:7 states, "How beautiful upon the mountains Are the *feet of him who brings good news*, Who proclaims peace, Who brings glad tidings of good things, Who proclaims salvation, Who says to Zion, 'Your God reigns!'" (emphasis added). Because of the good news, peace, glad tidings, and salvation that Jesus brought to Mary's life, she was in essence thanking Him with the most precious representations of her whole life—one full year of service required to buy the oil and the glory of her hair.

As kings in the marketplace, we too can honor the Lord in the same exact way by dedicating our entire work as worship unto Him and laying the crowns of our glory found in our work at His feet. In so doing, we give the Lord glory and honor and thanks as spoken about in Revelation 4:9–11, "Whenever the living creatures give glory and honor and thanks to Him who sits on the throne, who lives forever and ever, the twenty-four elders fall down before Him who sits on the throne and worship Him who lives forever and ever, and *cast their crowns before the throne*, saying: 'You are worthy, O Lord, To receive glory and honor and power; For You created all things, And by Your will they exist and were created'" (emphasis added). There is no greater glory we can give the Lord than to lay down our entire lives at His feet in true worship and thanks for what He has done for us on the cross.

THE KINGDOM'S CULTURE OF EMPOWERMENT

On a visit to New York City, I had the pleasure of visiting Trinity Episcopal Church to see the cross that was made from a sectional beam of the World Trade Center, discovered among the 9/11 wreckage. My understanding is that this cross will be prominently displayed as a monument at the foot of the new Freedom Tower being erected in place of the former twin World Trade towers. Think about the significance of a cross planted as a monument in the epicenter of Wall Street and the Freedom Tower of world trade. What a powerful representation of the freedom we find in the Cross of our Lord and Savior, Jesus Christ, and its impact on the world stage.

In fact, it is recorded in Luke 4:17–21, where Jesus reads from the Book of Isaiah and declares the freedom that He was anointed to bring to the world:

> And He [Jesus] was handed the book of the prophet Isaiah. And when He had opened the book, He found the place where it was written:
> "The Spirit of the LORD is upon Me, Because He has anointed Me To preach the gospel to the poor; He has sent Me to heal the brokenhearted, To proclaim liberty to the captives And recovery of sight to the blind, To set at liberty those who are oppressed; To proclaim the acceptable year of the LORD."
> Then He closed the book, and gave it back to the attendant and sat down. And the eyes of all who were in the synagogue were fixed on Him. And He began to say to them, "Today this Scripture is fulfilled in your hearing."

Personally, I believe that the Lord has anointed kings in His kingdom to do the same thing, bringing the good news of the gospel to our marketplaces and creating cultures of empowerment in every sphere of influence on earth. In his book, *Church in the Workplace*, C. Peter Wagner identifies what he calls The Seven Molders of Culture—family, religion, government, media, education, business, and the arts—and states in his own words:

Each should be seen as an apostolic sphere, requiring apostolic leadership to transform that unit into a society that reflects the values and lifestyle of the kingdom of God. Not only that, but consider the fact that each of these molders of culture and each significant subdivision will have its own rule book. Only those immersed in the culture of that social unit will understand the rule book and know how to operate by its rules. They are the only ones who will be able to change the power structures at the top of each mountain.

Nuclear-church apostles can influence religion and, to a degree, family. But they have virtually no influence over the other five molders of culture. Only extended-church apostles will be able to lead the army of God into those strategic battlefields.[1]

As a matter of definition and clarification, what C. Peter Wagner refers to in his quoted writing as nuclear-church apostles, I am referring to as priests in this book context and what he refers to as extended-church apostles in his quoted writing, I am referring to as kings in this book context.

THE KING'S RULE BOOK FOR THE BUSINESS MOLDER OF CULTURE

As a matter of principle, I believe living life on purpose is a personal choice as well as a personal privilege. In fact, Rick Warren's book *The Purpose Driven Life* has sold more copies than any other book in the history of the world with the exception of the Bible. Based on the unbelievable magnitude of his book's readership, it is quite clear and evident that God most certainly created people with an inherent desire to live life on purpose.

Now, while I believe living life on purpose is a noble choice and a great privilege, I also believe that living life with unified purpose is an even more noble choice and an even greater privilege. That's because one person choosing to live life on purpose may be able to accomplish a lot of good; however, many people choosing to live life with unified purpose can accomplish even greater good than just one person can working alone. It is a simple truth that no matter how great we might be individually, the sum of all of us is always exponentially greater when working together with unified purpose.

In Ecclesiastes 3:1 the Bible states, "To everything there is a season, A time for every purpose under heaven"; therefore, we can find comfort knowing that each of us have specific purpose and value in God's kingdom. Plus, organizations comprised of people are also especially designed by God with specific purpose and value through corporate unity. Ecclesiastes 4:12 specifically affirms that there is strength in unified corporate purpose, stating, "Though one may be overpowered by another, two can withstand him, And a threefold cord is not easily broken." The way that organizations become strengthened in corporate purpose is through unified support for the values of the organization—team values unify team purpose. And the principle is the same in the kingdom of God—kingdom values unify kingdom purpose, as affirmed in Ezra 3:1, "And when the seventh month had come, and the children of Israel were in the cities, *the people gathered together as one man to Jerusalem*" (emphasis added).

Therefore, in order for the body of Christ to actually transform cultures into a society that corporately reflects and supports the values of the kingdom of God, the values of the kingdom of God must be effectively communicated in the language and cultural framework of the seven different molders of culture that C. Peter Wagner writes about in his book *The Church In The Workplace*. Mr. Wagner refers to this communication as "the rule book" of the specific culture and emphasizes that only those extended-church apostles who are completely immersed in those specific respective cultures will be able to understand the culture's rule book and know how to operate by its rules. As such, they will be the kingdom ambassadors that are uniquely equipped to effectively bridge the gap and transform each specific culture into a society that reflects the values and lifestyles of the kingdom of God.[2] I wholeheartedly agree with Mr. Wagner's conclusion on this matter.

As an ambassador of the Lord's kingdom in the marketplace with twenty years of business and professional leadership experience as well as a Master's of Business Administration degree, an undergraduate finance degree, and a certified public accountant (inactive), I am well versed in the language and culture of the business world. Additionally, being a born-again believer for the past twenty years, I am equally well-versed in the values and lifestyle of the kingdom of God as demonstrated and taught by the Word of God.

With all of that said, I believe the Lord has specifically called me to be an extended-church apostle to the business community, one of the seven molders of modern-day culture as identified by Mr. Wagner. In fact, God has already led me, more than five years ago, to write my first faith-based business team values book entitled *The Make It Happen Journey*. In this book, specifically written for a business-based audience, I share nine kingdom-based team values which I call Make It Happen Team Values ©, respecting what I believe to be the "make it happen" business language of modern-day business culture as well as representing the "can do" faith values of the kingdom of God.

With twenty years of experience in the business world, I have learned that business people most certainly speak, think, and act in terms of a "make it happen" language and mentality. Additionally, as a serious, disciplined student of the Word of God for the first seven years of my faith journey with the Lord, I learned the "can do" faith values of the kingdom of God and was able to effectively teach, share, and reflect those values in the building and shaping of a "Make It Happen" business team. The Make It Happen Journey was written for business leaders to conceptualize the nine Make It Happen Team Values© that shaped and transformed the culture of my business team into a team that I believe reflects a "can do"culture of the Lord's kingdom empowerment in the business world. Bridging the communication gap between the values of the kingdom of God and the cultural language of business, Philippians 4:13 can read as, "I can do all things [make it happen] through Christ who strengthens me."

And as one would hopefully understand, because *The Make It Happen Journey* was intended to reach a business-based audience that includes a totally diverse population of people groups, ethnicities, and backgrounds of faith within the employee composite of American corporations versus an exclusively faith-based Christian audience, the book is carefully written in terms that maintain respect for the wide variety of stakeholders and audiences within the corporate business culture.

In addition to *The Make It Happen Journey* being a great kingdom resource for the business culture rule book, other kingdom resources are available from www.makeithappenbooks. com, the leadership reference library of The Make It Happen Learning Institute—Reaching People, Unleashing The Extraordinary!® From www.makeithappenbooks.com, a kingdom business leader can subscribe to The Make It Happen Learning Institute's free monthly faith-based leadership education e-mail

Kings Come Forth!

series, The Make It Happen Moment®, as well as purchase other excellent leadership education books officially endorsed by The Make It Happen Learning Institute as Make It Happen Books™.

The whole purpose of The Make It Happen Learning Institute is to reach people in the marketplace and unleash their extraordinary God-given potential to make a difference in life with kingdom principles that take the marketplace for the kingdom of God. The strategic operating plan that God has given me to effectively do this includes the establishment of Make It Happen Leadership Development Colleges in businesses all across America. In the format of a small group leadership development book club, a Make It Happen Leadership Development College is especially designed to coach, mentor, and develop business leaders in the marketplace within a framework of faith-based leadership principles that bridge the gap to the operating rule book of the business culture. In essence, the legal and operating structure of the Make It Happen Leadership Development Colleges has been created to allow for Bible believing business leaders of the kingdom to effectively teach and disciple other business leaders in the business marketplace in how to be effective kings in the kingdom. However, the bridge between the two offered by this new discipleship paradigm will require the church to face its fears and embrace the apostolic authority of a new, up-and-coming breed of extended-church apostles in the business world.

THE KING'S FIGHT TO WIN WITH INTEGRITY IN THE MARKETPLACE

Do you remember the movie *Rocky II* when Rocky's heart wasn't in the fight because his wife, Adrian, didn't want him to get back in the arena with Apollo Creed? Rocky's personal trainer, Mickey, couldn't quite understand what was wrong with Rocky and why he wasn't training to win. It wasn't until Adrian, after coming out of a coma in the hospital, whispered into Rocky's ear to go and "win" that Rocky got his motivation back to enter the fight and train to win. At that moment, an elated Mickey shouted, "What are we waiting for?" and the real training began![3]

I personally think the kings in the marketplace are responding to their opportunity to get in the kingdom arena and fight to win much like Rocky was doing before his partner in life released him to get in the ring and fight to win. In the Scriptures, there is an odd sequence of verses where Jesus is speaking of John the Baptist as well as the violent fight in the kingdom of God. In Matthew 11:12–17, it is recorded:

> And from the days of John the Baptist until now the kingdom of heaven suffers violence, and the violent take it by force. For all the prophets and the law prophesied until John. And if you are willing to receive it, he is Elijah who is to come. He who has ears to hear, let him hear! But to what shall I liken this generation? It is like children sitting in the marketplaces and calling to their companions, and saying: "We played the flute for you, And you did not dance; We mourned to you, And you did not lament."

In these verses it is clear that Jesus describes a fight that is taking place in the kingdom of God; however, as kings in the marketplace, we must understand that our fight for the kingdom is not against flesh and blood, but is rather a spiritual fight that we are destined to win in the kingdom of God. Ephesians 6:12 states, "For we do not wrestle against flesh and blood, but against principalities, against powers, against the rulers of the darkness of this age, against spiritual hosts of wickedness in the heavenly places." Therefore, to transform business culture into a society that reflects the values and lifestyle of the kingdom of God, kings must fight the battle on their knees, praying, fasting, and being the spiritual kingdom of light that violently pushes back the spiritual kingdom of darkness by the way we live our kingdom values in the business marketplace. This can only be done by the power and might of the Holy Spirit living in us and empowering us to take the kingdom of God to every sphere of influence on earth.

However, as I've stated throughout this book, I don't think the Lord expects us to fight this battle alone. I believe that He expects kings to fight the battle with the support, encouragement, and spiritual covering of priests—our kingdom life partners—just like the model established by King Hezekiah when he sent out kings and priests together to establish the kingdom in the cities. In fact, even Jesus did the same thing when He sent out the apostles two-by-two into the dark cities as lambs among wolves. Luke 10:1–3 records how the Lord intended for his apostles to take the kingdom of God into the cities of the land:

> After these things the Lord appointed seventy others also, and sent them two by two before His face into every city and place where He Himself was about to go. Then He said to them, "The harvest truly is great, but the laborers are few; therefore pray the Lord of the harvest to send out laborers into His harvest. Go your way; behold, I send you out as lambs among wolves."

I believe it is clear that the kingdom cannot and will not be won in every sphere of influence until the kings and priests of the kingdom spiritually partner together to fight the battle with both hands fully functioning, healthy and well.

Unfortunately, though, until now I think the partnership between kings and priests can be best characterized by the odd scripture verses that Jesus spoke regarding John the Baptist and the spiritual battle in the kingdom of God. In those verses He likens the generation to *"children sitting in the marketplaces and calling to their companions,* and saying: 'We played the flute for you, And you did not dance; We mourned to you, And you did not lament'" (Matt. 11:16–17, emphasis added). Notice how he points out children sitting in the marketplaces calling out to their companions. I believe this could relate to the current state of partnership between kings and priests where the kings are sitting idle in the marketplace waiting and looking for the priests to partner with them as kingdom dance partners in every sphere of influence—but it's just not happening as God intends for it to be.

So my prophetic question is this: How long is the church going to embrace a divided kingdom of priests and kings, afraid to release the kings to enter the fight to win the kingdom of God with integrity in the marketplace? The prophet of God in me is shouting like Mickey, "What are we waiting for?" while the king in me is patiently waiting on the Lord to whisper to the priests of the kingdom to in turn whisper to the kings of the kingdom and say, "Stretch out your hand, go, and win!"

Such support and encouragement from their God-designed kingdom life partners will give kings in the kingdom the assurances and motivation they need, knowing that their spiritual backs are covered and that it is OK to fight and win with integrity for the kingdom of God in the marketplaces of our world. When that happens, the kings will train to win and fight like mighty warriors in the power and might of the Holy Spirit to take the ground for the kingdom of the Lord in partnership with the priests. With a perfect kingdom partnership of kings and priests working perfectly together in a spirit of unity, it won't take long before the angels of the Lord in Revelation 11:5 (KJV) are singing, "The kingdoms of this world are become the kingdoms of our Lord, and of His Christ; and He shall reign for ever and ever." Hallelujah and amen!

8

The Soon-Coming King of Kings

Now therefore, be wise, O kings; Be instructed,
you judges of the earth. Serve the LORD with
fear, And rejoice with trembling. Kiss the Son,
lest He be angry, And you perish in the way,
When His wrath is kindled a little. Blessed
are all those who put their trust in Him.

—Psalm 2:10–12

CAPTIVATED BY GOD'S KINGDOM VISION

By now, having read through the previous seven chapters, I pray
that the Lord has sincerely captivated your heart with God-
ordained purpose for His kingdom on earth and in heaven.
That's because Jesus has promised that He will one day soon
return to earth to establish His kingdom reign with you and
me for one thousand years, and I want you to be ready. This
kingdom truth is firmly established by the Word of God in
Revelation 5:10, stating, "And [the Lord] have made us kings
and priests to our God; and we shall reign on the earth," and
Revelation 20:6, stating, "Blessed and holy is he who has part in
the first resurrection. Over such the second death has no power,
but they shall be priests of God and of Christ, and shall reign
with Him a thousand years."

Now, I know it sounds too incredible to be true, but it is
true; therefore, we must ask ourselves a very serious question in
light of this truth. When the Lord returns to earth in His glory,

what will He find His kings and priests doing? By His grace may He find you and me loving Him with our whole being and fulfilling our purpose in His kingdom by doing exactly what He has specifically called us to do with our gifts and talents—saving souls and building the kingdom of God for His glory and honor.

In Chip Ingram's book *Good to Great in God's Eyes*, Chip states, "It doesn't matter if you are seven or seventy; your heart should be captivated by a vision of how to serve God and accomplish something for His kingdom."[1] After all, the simple truth is that we were created to have a loving relationship with our heavenly Father and to accomplish something with our lives for His kingdom in complete worship of Him as our Lord and Savior. Jesus affirms this by stating in Matthew 22:37–39 that all the commandments of the Law and the prophets can be summed up into two great commandments: "'You shall love the LORD your God with all your heart, with all your soul, and with all your mind.' This is the first and great commandment. And the second is like it: 'You shall love your neighbor as yourself.'" When we do these two things, we actually reflect to the world around us the perfect kingdom of God living inside of us—the priest in us wholeheartedly loving God with everything that we are in Him and the king in us steadfastly building His kingdom in every sphere of influence, loving our neighbors as ourselves.

Now, understanding that God has especially designed a specific purpose for each of us to fulfill on earth should not at all be confused with the free gift of salvation in Christ Jesus that we receive by grace through faith—*not* by any work of our own accomplishment. That's because while we have all been created with purpose to accomplish something specific in God's kingdom, there is absolutely no amount of accomplishment that we can achieve that will purchase or earn our salvation in Christ.

The work of the Cross that Jesus accomplished at Calvary two thousand years ago is the only work that is holy and acceptable to God for the payment of our sins and the purchase of our salvation. When Jesus said "It is finished," it was completely and totally finished—no additional work required.

However, while our salvation is the free gift of grace and requires no additional sacrifice on our part to receive it, make no mistake about it, what we do with our redeemed lives in Christ does indeed matter intensely to God. If our eternal salvation is the only thing that mattered to God, then as soon as we believe in Jesus, He would just zap us up into heaven and take us home to be with Him. Obviously this doesn't happen, so there must be something more to our faith than just our eternal salvation in Christ. And there is—it's called worship in the form of a living sacrifice.

The apostle Paul defines this kind of worship in Romans 12:1, stating, "I beseech you therefore, brethren, by the mercies of God, that you present your bodies a living sacrifice, holy, acceptable to God, which is your reasonable *service*" (emphasis added). The word *service* in this verse is translated from the original Greek word *latreian* which means divine service or worship.[2] This means that whatever we do each day of our lives, we should do it as worship unto our Lord; otherwise, our "faith without works is dead," as declared by the apostle James in chapter 2, verse 20 of his epistle. In other words, our works in the Lord put feet on our faith and demonstrate to the world that the Lord is alive and well and His kingdom is at hand.

THE KINGDOM VISION: THY KINGDOM COME, THY WILL BE DONE ON EARTH AS IT IS IN HEAVEN

Besides the apostle Paul telling us to do everything in the kingdom as worship unto God in divine service to Him, Paul teaches us how to prove what is the good, acceptable, perfect will of God in our lives, stating in Romans 12:2, "And do not be conformed to this world, but be transformed by the renewing of your mind, that you may prove what is that good and acceptable and perfect *will* of God" (emphasis added). Considering that Paul tells us that we can prove the perfect will of God in our lives, and knowing from the Scriptures that Jesus prayed for God's kingdom to come and His *will* to be done on earth as it is in heaven, two things are clear to me about the perfect will of God and His kingdom on earth: (1) the perfect will of God originates in us by our thoughts and actions, and (2) the perfect kingdom of God happens on earth when our thoughts line up with His perfect will to the degree that our actions begin to reflect the Lord's kingdom in our everyday choices. This kingdom life process can be better explained by what I call The Life Cycle of Words.

THE LIFE CYCLE OF WORDS

I firmly believe that we must *think* kingdom thoughts, if we are going to *see* kingdom life in our everyday spheres of influence. By taking "every thought captive to the obedience of Christ," as Paul teaches in 2 Corinthians 10:5, we harness the creative power of God to build His kingdom in us and through us in our everyday lives, as well as leave a kingdom legacy of righteous living along the way. Our ability to transform our everyday lives as well as the everyday cultures of society all begins with the words we embrace and think. And that's because:

+ Words create thoughts.

+ Thoughts produce feelings.

+ Feelings inspire choices.

+ Choices generate actions.

+ Actions determine habits.

+ Habits develop character.

+ Character fulfills destiny.

+ Destiny breeds legacy.

Simply put, the power of life, destiny, and legacy is in the power of our words. Proverbs 23:7 states, "For as he thinks in his heart, so is he" and Proverbs 18:21 states, "Death and life are in the power of the tongue, And those who love it will eat its fruit." Therefore, it is absolutely clear that the words we speak and think will actually become the life we live, the destiny we fulfill, and the legacy we leave. This is why we must develop a daily loving relationship with the living Word of God if we desire to live the abundant blessed life and leave a righteous kingdom legacy in our families and in our communities. God's kingdom life happens in us and through us when we embrace God's kingdom Word and do it—it's just that simple.

THE FAITHFUL KINGDOM SERVANT

So if kingdom life is as simple as embracing God's Word and just doing it, then why don't we see more of His kingdom operating in our own lives and the world around us? It's a good question that I believe can be answered by studying His Word regarding the parable of the talents recorded in Matthew 25:14–30:

For the kingdom of heaven is like a man traveling to a far country, who called his own servants and delivered his goods to them. And to one he gave five talents, to another two, and to another one, to each according to his own ability; and immediately he went on a journey. Then he who had received the five talents went and traded with them, and made another five talents. And likewise he who had received two gained two more also. But he who had received one went and dug in the ground, and hid his lord's money. After a long time the lord of those servants came and settled accounts with them.

So he who had received five talents came and brought five other talents, saying, "Lord, you delivered to me five talents; look, I have gained five more talents besides them." His lord said to him, "Well done, good and faithful servant; you were faithful over a few things, I will make you ruler over many things. Enter into the joy of your lord." He also who had received two talents came and said, "Lord, you delivered to me two talents; look, I have gained two more talents besides them." His lord said to him, "Well done, good and faithful servant; you have been faithful over a few things, I will make you ruler over many things. Enter into the joy of your lord." Then he who had received the one talent came and said, "Lord, I knew you to be a hard man, reaping where you have not sown, and gathering where you have not scattered seed. And I was afraid, and went and hid your talent in the ground. Look, there you have what is yours." But his lord answered and said to him, "You wicked and lazy servant, you knew that I reap where I have not sown, and gather where I have not scattered seed. So you ought to have deposited my money with the bankers, and at my coming I would have received back my own with interest. So take the talent from him, and give it to him who has ten talents. For to everyone who has, more will be given, and he will have abundance; but from him who does not have, even what he has will be taken away. And cast the unprofitable servant into the outer darkness. There will be weeping and gnashing of teeth."

I believe this parable of the talents that Jesus shared with His disciples provides significant insight into why we don't see more of God's kingdom influence in us and in the world around us. The bottom line is that it's basically a kingdom stewardship issue. Remember in Genesis when the Lord spoke to Adam and Eve and commanded them to be fruitful, multiply, subdue, and have dominion? He was basically telling them that the kingdom was theirs, but they would have to obey His Word, take care of His kingdom, and increase it through His blessing and His gifts to them. There are no two ways about it—God's kingdom is a kingdom of blessing, gifts, and increase; however, we are the stewards who must faithfully invest our gifts and talents from the Lord to build the kingdom and increase it in every sphere of dominion influence. If it doesn't happen, it's not because God doesn't want it to happen. It's simply because we don't make it happen as His faithful stewards on the earth.

Unfortunately, I think many of God's people are like the wicked lazy servant who took his talent, buried it in the ground, and was afraid to step out in faith to make something happen for his lord. God has given each of us gifts and talents to be invested in His kingdom for multiplied return. If we don't do it, it's not the Lord's fault, it's ours. And unfortunately, our lack of faith and laziness will cause us to lose our reward of ruler-ship that He desires to give us now on earth and upon His return. In Matthew 16:27 it is recorded, "For the Son of Man will come in the glory of His Father with His angels, and then He will reward each according to his works." Therefore, it is most definitely evident that this is serious kingdom business to the Lord. So let me ask this question again. What will the Lord find you doing when He returns in His glory—being a faithful steward of your gifts and talents like the two wise, faithful servants in the parable of the talents or wasting your gifts and talents like the lazy, wicked servant who buried his talents in the ground? It's a choice only you can make.

The Crown of Righteousness

For those faithful stewards who daily fight the good fight of faith, investing their gifts and talents in the kingdom of God, producing fruit in every area of stewardship—spiritual, social, mental, physical, and financial—there is a crown of righteousness reserved for them in heaven. The apostle Paul assures us of this in 2 Timothy 4:7–8, stating, "I have fought the good fight, I have finished the race, I have kept the faith. Finally, there is laid up for me the crown of righteousness, which the Lord, the righteous Judge, will give to me on that Day, and not to me only but also to all who have loved His appearing." Knowing that the Lord is soon returning with His reward in hand should inspire faithful stewards to do all that they can to build His kingdom in a manner that will cause Him to say, "Well done, thy good and faithful servant." How beautiful and sweet to the ears will be those seven little words uttered by our Lord as He gently places a crown of righteousness upon our heads.

Let us not be kings who go through life allowing fear to rob us of the joy of being good faithful stewards in the kingdom of God. Fearing what people may think of us if we assertively use our gifts and talents to influence our culture will certainly not cause us to lose our salvation; however, it can certainly cause us to lose our kingdom reward and enter heaven as a kingdom pauper. How sad would it be to watch other faithful stewards lay down their crowns of righteousness at the feet of our Lord in praise and worship to Him while having no crown of our own to lay at His feet? I share this vivid picture of what it would be like to be a kingdom pauper in the presence of our Lord to hopefully stir you into action as a faithful steward of the Lord's kingdom. In so doing, you shall be fully prepared when He soon returns in His Father's glory to reward His faithful kingdom stewards. Revelation 22:12–13 provides further encouragement, stating, "And behold, I [the Lord Jesus, King of kings] am coming quickly, and My reward is with Me, to give to every one according to his work. I am the Alpha and the Omega, the Beginning and the End, the First and the Last." All praise, glory, and honor to our Lord and Savior, forever and ever! Amen and amen!

SEE YOU AT THE OFFICE PRAYER MOVEMENT

Now that you have read Kings Come Forth!, it is my prayer that you are fully awakened by the Holy Spirit to the call for business leaders to build the kingdom of God in the business community in partnership with the priests of His kingdom. So then the next obvious question is where does this huge kingdom mandate in the business community begin? Well, it first begins with business leaders having the courage to answer the call in faith to be set apart as business leaders fully dedicated to building God's kingdom in the business community as the Lord's modern-day kingdom ambassadors on earth.

Secondly, it begins with prayer. Second Chronicles 7:14 states, "If My people who are called by My name will humble themselves, and pray and seek My face, and turn from their wicked ways, then I will hear from heaven, and will forgive their sin and heal their land." Simply put, the mandate communicated in this book to build God's kingdom in the business community is an impossible mandate…if the business leaders in God's kingdom do not first humble ourselves and pray. Therefore, in addition to the kingdom mandate that the Lord has compelled me to write in Kings Come Forth!, the Lord has been also impressing upon me to initiate a prayer movement led by business leaders in the business community called "See You At The Office" similar to the student led prayer movement called "See You At The Pole". If the students of our nation care enough about our nation and their schools to show up at the pole each year on a special day set apart to pray for their classmates, their schools, and our nation, how much more should the business leaders in our nation do the same? As such, in obedience to the Lord, it is my sincere pleasure to partner with you and all other caring business leaders to coordinate two days of prayer at the office each year during the week of July 14 as a special emphasis of God's promise in 2 Chronicles 7:14. (Note: two days during the week of July 14 each year.) I look forward to seeing you at the office!

☙

A BEGINNING PRAYER

Heavenly Father, I thank You for the magnificent privilege to come boldly before Your throne of grace as a man of God humbled by Your righteous judgments. As a king in Your kingdom, upheld by Your righteous right hand, I petition You with prayer and thanksgiving in my heart on behalf of all Your kings who seek to do Your will on earth as it is in heaven, fully knowing that You have brought us to the kingdom for such a time as this. Teach us, Lord, to count our days and be faithful stewards of the precious time and talents that You have given to each of us, redeeming the time on earth and building Your kingdom in the power and might of Your precious Holy Spirit. Grant us, Lord, a spirit of wisdom and excellence to seek first Your kingdom in everything we do, that we might fulfill the purposes of Your kingdom in our generation. Grant us, Lord, a spirit of faith and humility to love You with all of our heart, mind, and soul that we might become the people of Your pasture in our communities. And grant us, Lord, a spirit of generosity and commitment to love our neighbors as ourselves that we might become Your hands and feet to a hurting world. With forgiveness in our hearts, one to another, may the kings and priests of Your kingdom embrace grace and truth in a spirit of unity that will powerfully demonstrate Your perfect kingdom to the world around us in perfect harmony and love through You, our heavenly Father, Lord and Savior, King of kings. May Your kingdom light shine in us ever so brightly before all people to bless the nations with Your unfailing love and Your glorious, righteous rule, forever and ever. In Jesus' name I pray. Amen and amen!

Notes

INTRODUCTION

1. John W. Maxwell, *The Maxwell Leadership Bible* (Nashville, TN: Thomas Nelson, 2002).

CHAPTER 1
THE GREAT DISTINCTION OF KINGS

1. *Hitchcock's Bible Names Dictionary*, PC Study Bible, Biblesoft, Inc., 2003, 2006.

2. *Hitchcock's Bible Names Dictionary*, PC Study Bible, Biblesoft, Inc., 2003, 2006.

3. *Merriam-Webster's Collegiate Dictionary, Eleventh Edition* (Springfield, MA: 2003), s.v. "Anointed."

4. Ed Silvoso, *Anointed For Business* (Ventura, CA: Regal, 2002).

5. David Wilkerson, *Knowing God by Name* (Grand Rapids, MI: Chosen Books, 2003), 125.

6. Jessie Duplantis, *Everyday Visionary* (Austin, TX: Touchstone, 2008).

7. Mike Murdock, *The One Minute Business Man's Devotional* (Colorado Springs, CO: Honor Books, 1994), 126.

CHAPTER 2
THE SPIRITUAL ENVIRONMENT OF THE
CURRENT-DAY KINGDOM MARKETPLACE

1. Quote from Yogi Berra found at http://www.brainyquote. com/quotes/quotes/y/yogiberra125285.html (accessed October 27, 2010).

2. Article by Aaron Smith found at http://money.cnn.com/2008/09/26/news/companies/fishman_wamu/ (accessed October 24, 2010).

3. Figures from the Conference Board Survey, August 2004, found at website: http://www.peoplehrforum.com/index.php?view=tpl_topics_detail&topic_id=755&forum_id=201 (accessed October 27, 2010).

4. Declaration of Independence found in the National Archives at http://www.archives.gov/exhibits/charters/declaration_transcript.html (accessed October 26, 2010).

5. Ron DiCianni, *The Faith of the Presidents* (Lake Mary, FL: Charisma House, 2004).

6. Franklin Covey 1998 survey presentation, Distinguished Speaker Series: Lessons In Leadership, *Solving the Puzzle: How to Unleash Your Team's Potential.*

CHAPTER 3
THE THREE KINGDOM OFFICES OF GODLY SPIRITUAL AUTHORITY

1. *Easton's Bible Dictionary*, PC Study Bible, Biblesoft, Inc., 2003, 2006, s.vv. "priest," "prophet," "king."

CHAPTER 4
THE KING'S ANOINTING AND PURPOSE

1. Randy Alcorn. *Treasure Principle* (Sisters, OR: Multnomah, 2001).

2. DiCianni, *The Faith of the Presidents.*

3. John Bevere, *Honor's Reward* (Nashville, TN: FaithWords, 2007).

Chapter 5
The Kingdom Partnership

1. Dani Johnson, *Spirit Driven Success* (Shippensburg, PA: Destiny Image, 2009).

Chapter 6
The Restoration of Kings to the Kingdom Business

1. Doug Sherman and William Hendrick, *Your Work Matters to God* (Colorado Springs, CO: NavPress, 1987).

2. Quote from *Spider-Man* found at The Internet Movie Database Website http://www.imdb.com/title/tt0145487/quotes (accessed October 26, 2010).

3. John Maxwell, *The Power of Leadership* (Colorado Springs: David C. Cook, 2001).

Chapter 7
The Awakened Kingdom Mandate

1. C. Peter Wagner, *Church in the Workplace* (Ventura, CA: Regal, 2006).

2. Ibid.

3. Information on *Rocky* found at The Internet Movie Database Website http://www.imdb.com/title/tt0075148/ (accessed October 26, 2010).

Chapter 8
The Soon Coming King of Kings

1. Chip Ingram, *Good to Great in God's Eyes* (Grand Rapids, MI: Baker, 2007).

2. *Merriam-Webster's Collegiate Dictionary, Eleventh Edition* (Springfield, MA: 2003).

About the Author

GARY J. BORGSTEDE is the husband of a beautiful wife, the father of five wonderful children, a business executive, a published author, a national speaker, and a pastor actively engaged in reaching people and building lives through the ministry of his local church. From the parking lot ministry, prison ministry, and men's ministry, Gary is fully committed to the cause of Jesus Christ to reach people and build lives through the unconditional love of God. As the president and founder of The Make It Happen Learning Institute, Gary specifically seeks to fulfill the call of God on his life to effectively equip business leaders in building the kingdom of God in the business marketplace. By reaching people in the marketplace, unleashing their extraordinary God-given potential to make a difference in life, and advancing the kingdom of God for His glory in the business community, it is Gary's prayer that modern-day kings—business leaders in the community—will fulfill their destinies in God as anointed business leaders in the kingdom of our Lord and Savior, Jesus Christ, the King of kings and Lord of lords. In 2009, Gary left his vice president role at Ochsner Health System to join the leadership team at Church of the King in Mandeville, Louisiana, as the chief administrative officer and pastor of business leaders in the marketplace.

About The Make It Happen Learning Institute

Reaching People, Unleashing the Extraordinary!®

The Make It Happen Learning Institute is a faith-based business leadership development organization founded by Gary J. Borgstede to develop godly business leaders in the marketplace and equip them to advance the kingdom of God in business through faith-based team values that reach people and unleash their extraordinary God-given potential to make a difference in life. To help fulfill this vision, Gary has written the business leadership book *The Make It Happen Journey*, which highlights the faith-based Make It Happen Team Values that he has taught and lived as a business executive with his own business teams in corporate America. By living and teaching Make It Happen Team Values to the members of his own team, Gary has been able to successfully build team cultures of kingdom empowerment that glorify God, serve others, and empower people to fulfill their purpose in God and make a real difference in life.

In addition to *The Make It Happen Journey*, Gary's second business leadership book, *Kings Come Forth!*, is written to inspire and encourage business leaders in the marketplace (modern-day kings) to awaken their spiritual destinies in God and advance the kingdom of God in business with faith-based values and leadership principles from the Word of God. To help business leaders effectively do this, The Make It Happen Learning Institute offers business executives the opportunity to host an onsite Make It Happen Leadership Development College at their company in the format of a monthly small group book club led by a company facilitator certified by The Make It Happen Learning Institute. Furthermore, The Make It Happen Learning Institute provides business leaders in the marketplace with free faith-based leadership education through The Make It Happen Moment®, written by Gary and distributed on a monthly basis via e-mail subscription. And lastly, the leadership reference library of The Make It Happen Learning Institute is available online at www.makeithappenboooks.com for the purchase of trusted leadership books officially endorsed by The Make It Happen Learning Institute as Make It Happen Books™.

ॐ

The Make It Happen Books logo is a registered trademark of The Make It Happen Learning Institute.

Contact the Author

To LEARN MORE about how you and your team can take advantage of The Make It Happen Learning Institute's leadership development opportunities, please visit us at www.makeithappenlearninginstitute.com or write to:

The Make It Happen Learning Institute
Attention: Gary J. Borgstede
P. O. Box 355
Madisonville, LA 70477

To receive The Make It Happen Learning Institute's periodic faith-based leadership educational e-mail message, *The Make It Happen Moment*®, please visit www.makeithappenbooks.com, the on-line leadership reference library of The Make It Happen Learning Institute, to subscribe.